First World War
and Army of Occupation
War Diary
France, Belgium and Germany

41 DIVISION
Divisional Troops
Royal Army Service Corps
299 Company ASC
4 May 1916 - 30 September 1919

WO95/2631/6

The Naval & Military Press Ltd
www.nmarchive.com
Published in association with The National Archives

Published by

The Naval & Military Press Ltd

Unit 10 Ridgewood Industrial Park,

Uckfield, East Sussex,

TN22 5QE England

Tel: +44 (0) 1825 749494

www.naval-military-press.com

www.nmarchive.com

This diary has been reprinted in facsimile from the original. Any imperfections are inevitably reproduced and the quality may fall short of modern type and cartographic standards.

© Crown Copyright
Images reproduced by permission of The National Archives, London, England, 2015.

Contents

Document type	Place/Title	Date From	Date To
Heading	WO95/2631/6 299 Coy ASC		
Heading	41 Div. Train 299 Coy ASC 1916 May-1917 Oct 1918 Mar-1919 Sept Italy 1917 Nov-1918 Feb		
War Diary	Mytchett	04/05/1916	04/05/1916
War Diary	Havre	05/05/1916	06/05/1916
War Diary	Haze-Brouck	07/05/1916	07/05/1916
War Diary	Wallon. Cappell	08/05/1916	09/05/1916
War Diary	Outer-Steen	10/05/1916	31/05/1916
War Diary	La Creche	01/06/1916	30/06/1916
War Diary	Mytchett	04/05/1916	04/05/1916
War Diary	Havre	05/05/1916	06/05/1916
War Diary	Haze-Brouck	07/05/1916	07/05/1916
War Diary	Wallon Cappell	08/05/1916	09/05/1916
War Diary	Outer-Steen.	10/05/1916	31/05/1916
War Diary		01/07/1916	14/07/1916
War Diary	La Creche	15/07/1916	17/07/1916
War Diary	Les Trois Fermes Outersteen	18/07/1916	22/07/1916
War Diary	Long	23/08/1916	06/09/1916
War Diary	St Sauveur	07/07/1916	07/07/1916
War Diary	Buire	08/09/1916	11/09/1916
War Diary	1 Mile South Of Albert	12/09/1916	18/09/1916
War Diary	Buire L2D/D 30 B 4.1	19/09/1916	30/09/1916
War Diary	Buire	01/10/1916	01/10/1916
War Diary	Becordel	02/10/1916	13/10/1916
War Diary	Buire	14/10/1916	16/10/1916
War Diary	Argoeuves	17/10/1916	17/10/1916
War Diary	Airaines	18/10/1916	19/10/1916
War Diary	Caistre	20/10/1916	20/10/1916
War Diary	Pinchoon	21/10/1916	21/10/1916
War Diary	Reninghelst	22/10/1916	31/10/1916
War Diary	Reninghelst G 34	01/11/1916	30/11/1916
War Diary	Reninghelst G 34	08/11/1916	15/11/1916
War Diary	Reninghelst	01/12/1916	21/03/1917
War Diary	Steenvorde	22/03/1917	06/04/1917
War Diary	Reninghelst.	07/04/1917	16/05/1917
War Diary	Noordpeene	17/05/1917	17/05/1917
War Diary	Salperwick	18/05/1917	31/05/1917
War Diary	Renninghelst	01/06/1917	12/06/1917
War Diary	Ouderdom	13/06/1917	19/06/1917
War Diary	Reninghelst	20/06/1917	30/06/1917
War Diary	Fontaine Huick	01/07/1917	17/07/1917
War Diary	Westoutre	18/07/1917	24/07/1917
War Diary	Reninghelst	25/07/1917	14/08/1917
War Diary	Thieushouk	15/08/1917	24/08/1917
War Diary	Staple	25/08/1917	25/08/1917
War Diary	Scaderbourg	26/08/1917	31/08/1917
War Diary	St Martin Au-Laert	01/09/1917	13/09/1917
War Diary	St Marie Cappel	14/09/1917	14/09/1917
War Diary	Thieushouk	15/09/1917	15/09/1917
War Diary	Millekruisse	16/09/1917	21/09/1917

War Diary	Borre	22/09/1917	26/09/1917
War Diary	Wormhoudt	27/09/1917	27/09/1917
War Diary	Ghyvelde	28/09/1917	05/10/1917
War Diary	Stidesbalde	06/10/1917	27/10/1917
War Diary	Leffrinchouke	28/10/1917	31/10/1917
War Diary	Villa Franca	01/03/1918	01/03/1918
War Diary	In Farm	02/03/1918	05/03/1918
War Diary	Warluzel	06/03/1918	19/03/1918
War Diary	Louvencourt	20/03/1918	20/03/1918
War Diary	Lavieville	21/03/1918	21/03/1918
War Diary	Achiet-Le Petit	22/03/1918	24/03/1918
War Diary	Bienvillers Au-Bois	25/03/1918	25/03/1918
War Diary	St Amand	25/03/1918	25/03/1918
War Diary	Bailleulval	26/03/1918	27/03/1918
War Diary	Saulty	28/03/1918	28/03/1918
War Diary	Authies	29/03/1918	01/04/1918
War Diary	Famechon	02/04/1918	02/04/1918
War Diary	Petit Houvin	03/04/1918	03/04/1918
War Diary	Steenvorde	04/04/1918	06/04/1918
War Diary	Vlamertinghe	07/04/1918	08/04/1918
War Diary	Esterhoek	09/04/1918	25/04/1918
War Diary	Peselhoek Area	26/04/1918	26/04/1918
War Diary	Proven Area	27/04/1918	30/04/1918
War Diary	Proven Area Camp. N	01/05/1918	31/05/1918
War Diary	Camp N Sheet 27 F 2 7 A	01/06/1918	02/06/1918
War Diary	Bolezeele	03/06/1918	03/06/1918
War Diary	Brouere	04/06/1918	08/06/1918
War Diary	Hericat	09/06/1918	09/06/1918
War Diary	Bonningues	10/06/1918	24/06/1918
War Diary	Broere	25/06/1918	25/06/1918
War Diary	Ouderzeele	26/06/1918	30/06/1918
War Diary	Steenvorde	01/07/1918	06/09/1918
War Diary	Wippenhoek	07/09/1918	13/09/1918
War Diary	Lederzeele	14/09/1918	14/09/1918
War Diary	Clerques	15/09/1918	25/09/1918
War Diary	Rubroucq	26/09/1918	26/09/1918
War Diary	Wippenhoek	27/09/1918	27/09/1918
War Diary	Brandhoek	28/09/1918	30/09/1918
War Diary	Voormozeele	01/10/1918	06/10/1918
War Diary	Poperinghe	07/10/1918	10/10/1918
War Diary	Hillhoek	11/10/1918	12/10/1918
War Diary	Ypres	13/10/1918	15/10/1918
War Diary	Dadizeele	16/10/1918	19/10/1918
War Diary	Moorseele	20/10/1918	20/10/1918
War Diary	Bisinghem	21/10/1918	28/10/1918
War Diary	Courtrai	29/10/1918	01/11/1918
War Diary	Sveveghem	02/11/1918	04/11/1918
War Diary	Deerlyck	05/11/1918	09/11/1918
War Diary	Ingoyghem	10/11/1918	10/11/1918
War Diary	Berkhem	11/11/1918	13/11/1918
War Diary	Nederbrakel	14/11/1918	17/11/1918
War Diary	Meerschvoorde	18/11/1918	19/11/1918
War Diary	Viane	20/11/1918	11/12/1918
War Diary	Enghien	12/12/1918	12/12/1918
War Diary	Hal	13/12/1918	13/12/1918
War Diary	Waterloo	14/12/1918	15/12/1918

War Diary	Genappe	16/12/1918	16/12/1918
War Diary	Brye	17/12/1918	17/12/1918
War Diary	Temploux	18/12/1918	18/12/1918
War Diary	Vezin	19/12/1918	19/12/1918
War Diary	Huy	20/12/1918	06/01/1919
War Diary	On Train	07/01/1919	07/01/1919
War Diary	Heumar	08/01/1919	12/05/1919
War Diary	Rosrath	13/05/1919	19/06/1919
War Diary	Overath	20/06/1919	30/06/1919
War Diary	Rosrath	01/07/1919	11/08/1919
War Diary	Hack	12/08/1919	30/09/1919

WO95/2631/6

299 Coy ASC

BEF

41 Div. Train

299 Coy ASC

1916 MAY — 1917 OCT

1918 MAR — 1919 SEPT

ITALY 1917 NOV — 1918 FEB

Army Form C. 2118

WAR DIARY
or
INTELLIGENCE SUMMARY
(Erase heading not required.)

1916 | **376**

Instructions regarding War Diaries and Intelligence Summaries are contained in F. S. Regs., Part II. and the Staff Manual respectively. Title Pages will be prepared in manuscript.

Place	Date	Hour	Summary of Events and Information	Remarks and references to Appendices
Mytchett	4-9-16	11-30	Left Mytchett Camp.	
		13-14	Entrained at Sqd Farnborough to LSW Station	
		15-30	Arrived Southampton Docks. Embarked on S.S. Hunterleft. Weather fine. No casualties.	O.M.
		20-30	Left quay.	
Havre	5 "	10-00	Arrived Havre.	
		13-30	Arrived No 1 Rest Camp. Weather stormy. No casualties.	R.M.
Havre	6 "	7-30	Left Rest Camp.	
		13-30	Entrained at Gare Marchandises HAVRE. Weather variable. No casualties.	R.M.
HAZE-BROUCK	7 "	11-00	Arrive HAZEBROUCK.	
		15-30	Arrived at billets at WALLON CAPPELL Weather stormy. No casualties.	R.M.
WALLON CAPPELL	8 "	15-00	Supply section working. Supply Baggage wagons collected from units. Weather wet. No casualties.	R.M.

1875 Wt. W593/826 1,000,000 4/15 J.B.C. & A. A.D.S.S./Forms/C. 2118.

WAR DIARY
or
INTELLIGENCE SUMMARY

(Erase heading not required.)

Army Form C. 2118

Instructions regarding War Diaries and Intelligence Summaries are contained in F. S. Regs., Part II. and the Staff Manual respectively. Title Pages will be prepared in manuscript.

Place	Date	Hour	Summary of Events and Information	Remarks and references to Appendices
WALLON CAPPELL	9/5/16	8.30	Left Billets. Refilled on route & new Billets at LES TROIS TILLEUS OUTERSTEEN. Weather very wet. No casualties	AMR
OUTER-STEEN.	10/5/16		Supply sector working. Weather fair. No casualties	AMR
do	11/5/16		Supply sector working. Weather fair. Casualties 2 oxygen & horses 3 mules ty 119 Field Amb. AMR	AMR
do	12/5/16		Supply "Baggage" sector working. Weather wet. No casualties	AMR
do	13/5/16		Supply sector working. Weather wet. No casualties	AMR
do	14/5/16		Supply sector working. Weather wet. No casualties	AMR
do	15/5/16		Supply "Baggage" sector working. Weather stormy. [illegible] cases of MR returned	AMR

Army Form C. 2118

WAR DIARY
or
INTELLIGENCE SUMMARY
(Erase heading not required.)

Instructions regarding War Diaries and Intelligence Summaries are contained in F. S. Regs., Part II. and the Staff Manual respectively. Title Pages will be prepared in manuscript.

Place	Date	Hour	Summary of Events and Information	Remarks and references to Appendices
OUTER-STEEN	16/5/16		Supply & Baggage Sections working. Weather fair. 3 pcoty cases of ill returned.	RMR
"	17/5/16		Supply & Baggage Section working. Weather fine. No casualties	RM
"	18/5/16		Supply & Baggage Section working. Weather v. hot. Cpl. ADDISON. G 104 field amb. to vacand.	RM.
"	19/5/16		Supply & Baggage Section working. Weather v. hot. No casualties	RM.
"	20/5/16		Supply Section working. Weather v. hot. No casualties	RM.
"	21 5/16		Supply Section working. Weather v. hot. No casualties	RMR
"	22/5/16		Supply & Baggage Section working. Weather v. hot, late thunderstorm. No casualties	RMR

1875 Wt. W593/826 1,000,000 4/15 J.B.C. & A. A.D.S.S./Forms/C.2118.

WAR DIARY
or
INTELLIGENCE SUMMARY
(Erase heading not required.)

Army Form C. 2118

Place	Date	Hour	Summary of Events and Information	Remarks and references to Appendices
OUTER-STEEN.	23/8/16		Supply wagons working. Stormy	Dr. Buck admitted hospital
"	24		Supply Section working. Stormy	Dr. COLLIER discharged of hospital
"	25		Supply Baggage Section working. Fine	Dr. BUCK discharged of hospital
"	26		Supply Section working. Fine.	No casualties
"	27		Supply Baggage Section working. Fine	do
"	28		Supply Section working. Fine	do
"	29		Supply Section working. Baggage do. rejoined unit for move. Fine	2/Lt HOLLARD + A/CPL WHITE J. admitted hospital

WAR DIARY
or
INTELLIGENCE SUMMARY
(Erase heading not required.)

Army Form C. 2118

Place	Date	Hour	Summary of Events and Information	Remarks and references to Appendices
OUTER-STEEN	30/5/16		Supply & Baggage Section working. Fine, to Showery	No casualties
do	31/5/16		Moved into billets at LA CRECHE relief en route. Fine	do
LA CRECHE	1/6/16		Supply Section working. Fine	do
"	2/6/16		Supply Section working. Fine	Sr Dr Clay admitted Field Amb.
"	3/6/16		Supply Section working. Fine	No casualties
"	4/6/16		Supply & Baggage Section working. Fine.	do
"	5/6/16		do. Very wet	do
"	6/6/16		do Showery	do
"	7/6/16		do Fine	do

Army Form C. 2118

WAR DIARY
or
INTELLIGENCE SUMMARY
(Erase heading not required.)

Place	Date	Hour	Summary of Events and Information	Remarks and references to Appendices
LA CRECHE	8/6/15		Usual Routine. Fine.	RMP
"	9		do do	RMP
	10		do do	RMP
	11		do stormy	RMP
	12		do Very wet	RMP
	13		do do	RMP
	14		do stormy	RMP
	15		do. Dull	RMP
	16		do Fine 2/Lt Holland + Gillilly returned to duty. No casualties	RMP
	17		do do	RMP
	18		do do	RMP
	19		do do	RMP

Army Form C. 2118

WAR DIARY
or
INTELLIGENCE SUMMARY
(Erase heading not required.)

November 4th Bn. Devon Regt (T.F.)

Instructions regarding War Diaries and Intelligence Summaries are contained in F. S. Regs., Part II. and the Staff Manual respectively. Title Pages will be prepared in manuscript.

Place	Date 1916	Hour	Summary of Events and Information		Remarks and references to Appendices
LA CRECHE	June 20		Usual Routine	Stormy	App
	21		do	Wet	App
	22		do	do	App
	23		do	Showery	App
	24		do	Fine	App
	25		do	do	App
	26		do	do	Dr Cartwright to 138 Field Ambulance	App
	27		do	Stormy	Sd Dr Storey & Dr Morley joined the Coy.	App
	28		do	Stormy	No Casualties	App
	29		do	Wet	Dr Cartwright discharged Hospl.	App
	30		do	do	No Casualties	App
			do	Fine	do	App

1375 Wt. W.593/826 1,000,000 4/15 J.B.C. & A. A.D.S.S./Forms/C. 2118.

Army Form C. 2118

WAR DIARY
or
INTELLIGENCE SUMMARY
(Erase heading not required.)

No 4 bept Li 29th Divn AsC — 299 Coy — Vol. 1

Instructions regarding War Diaries and Intelligence Summaries are contained in F. S. Regs., Part II. and the Staff Manual respectively. Title Pages will be prepared in manuscript.

Place	Date	Hour	Summary of Events and Information	Remarks and references to Appendices
Mytchett	4.5.14	11.30	Left Mytchett Camp.	
		13.14	Entrained at South Farnborough L&SW Station.	
		15.30	Arrived Southampton Docks, embarked on S.S. Huntsgulf. Weather fine. No casualties.	PMR
		20.30	Left Quay.	
Havre	5"	10.00	Arrived Havre.	
		13.30	Arrived No 1 Rest Camp. Weather stormy. No casualties.	PMR
Havre	6"	9.30	Left Rest Camp.	
		13.30	Entrained at Gare Marchandises HAVRE. Weather variable. No casualties.	PMR
HAZE-BROUCK	7"	11.00	Arrived HAZEBROUCK.	
		15.30	Arrived at billets at WALLON CAPPELL. Weather stormy. No casualties.	PMR
WALLON CAPPELL	8"	15.00	Supply Section working. Supply Baggage wagons collected from unit. Weather wet. No casualties.	PMR

1875 Wt. W593/826 1,000,000 4/15 J.B.C. & A. A.D.S.S./Forms/C. 2118.

WAR DIARY
or
INTELLIGENCE SUMMARY
(Erase heading not required.)

Army Form C. 2118

Instructions regarding War Diaries and Intelligence Summaries are contained in F.S. Regs., Part II. and the Staff Manual respectively. Title Pages will be prepared in manuscript.

Place	Date	Hour	Summary of Events and Information	Remarks and references to Appendices
WALLON CAPPELL	9/5/16	8.30	Left Billets. Refilled en route for new Billets at LES TROIS TILLEULS, OUTERSTEEN. Weather very wet. No casualties	RMR
OUTER-STEEN.	10/5/16		Supply section working. Weather fair. No casualties	RMR
do	11/5/16		Supply section working. Weather fair. Men. Casualties, 2 officers & horses 3 rations S by 139 Field Amb.	RMR
do	12/5/16		Supply Baggage section working. Weather wet. No Casualties	RMR
do	13/5/16		Supply Section working. Weather wet. No casualties	RMR
do	14/5/16		Supply Section working. Weather wet. No casualties	RMR
do	15/5/16		Supply Baggage section working. Weather stormy. 2 wagon cases of 115/16 returned	RMR

WAR DIARY
or
INTELLIGENCE SUMMARY
(Erase heading not required.)

Army Form C. 2118

Army Troop H: 2nd Div Near Ott...

Place	Date	Hour	Summary of Events and Information	Remarks and references to Appendices
OUTER-STEEN	16/5/16		Supply Baggage Section working. Weather fair.	RMR
"	17/5/16		Supply Baggage Section working. Weather fair.	RMR
"	18/5/16		Supply Baggage Section working. Weather v. hot. Cpl. ADDISON. 6109 Picked out for Funeral.	RMR
"	19/5/16		Supply Baggage Section working. Weather v. hot. no casualties	RMR
"	20/5/16		Supply Section working. Weather v. hot. no casualties	RMR
"	21/5/16		Supply Section working. Weather v. hot. no casualties	RMR
"	22/5/16		Supply & Baggage Section working. Weather v. hot, late Thunder storm. no casualties	RMR

Army Form C. 2118

WAR DIARY
or
INTELLIGENCE SUMMARY
(Erase heading not required.)

Instructions regarding War Diaries and Intelligence Summaries are contained in F. S. Regs., Part II. and the Staff Manual respectively. Title Pages will be prepared in manuscript.

Place	Date	Hour	Summary of Events and Information	Remarks and references to Appendices
OUTER-STEEN	23/5/16		Supply Wagons working. Stormy. Dr Buck admitted hospital.	
"	24/5/16		Supply Section working. Stormy. Dr Collier discharged fr hospital.	
"	25 "		Supply & Baggage Section working. Fine. Dr Buck discharged fr hospital.	
"	26.		Supply Section working. Fine. No Casualties.	
"	27.		Supply & Baggage Section working. Fine. do	
"	28.		Supply Section working. Fine. do	
"	29.		Supply Section working. Baggage do rejoined unit for move. Fine. L. Holland, Sgt Whyte–J. admitted hospital. Fine.	

1875 Wt. W593/826 1,000,000 4/15 J.B.C. & A. A.D.S.S./Forms/C. 2118.

WAR DIARY
or
INTELLIGENCE SUMMARY
(Erase heading not required.)

Army Form C. 2118

Place	Date	Hour	Summary of Events and Information	Remarks and references to Appendices
OUTER-STEEN.	30/5/16		Supply Baggage Section Working. Fine & Showery	May be by 4th Div J. Mann Off. No Casualties
"	31/5/16		Moved into billets at LA CRECHE. Fine. Refilled en route.	do

Army Form C. 2118

WAR DIARY
or
INTELLIGENCE SUMMARY
(Erase heading not required.)

Instructions regarding War Diaries and Intelligence Summaries are contained in F. S. Regs., Part II. and the Staff Manual respectively. Title Pages will be prepared in manuscript.

Place	Date	Hour	Summary of Events and Information	Remarks and references to Appendices
JULY	1		Usual Routine Fine No Casualties	AM
	2		do do do	AM
	3		do Stormy do	PM
	4		do do do	PM
	5		do Wet do	PM
	6		do Wet Dr BENNETT transferred to 140 Field Ambulance	PM
	7		do Fine Dr CHARLES T.G. posted to this unit	PM
	8		do Fine No Casualties	PM
	9		do Showery Dr COX T admitted to 138 Field Amb.	PPR
	10		do Stormy No Casualties	PPR
	11		do Stormy do	PPR
	12		do Fine do	PPR
	13		do do do	PPR
	14		do do Dr COX T returned to duty.	PM

1375 Wt. W593/826 1,000,000 4/15. J.B.C. & A. A.D.S.S./Forms/C. 2118.

WAR DIARY
or
INTELLIGENCE SUMMARY
(Erase heading not required.)

Army Form C. 2118

Place	Date	Hour	Summary of Events and Information	Remarks and references to Appendices
LA CRECHE	15		Usual Routine	Fine	DRS RAINE & MORLEY W.H. admitted 138 Field Amb
	16		do	do	No casualties
	17		do	do	do
	18		do	do	DR STANDLEY J posted to this unit
	19		do	do	DR MORLEY W.H. returned to duty
	20		do	do	No casualties
	21		do	do	DR SANDFORD admitted 138 Field Amb.
	22		do	do	No Casualties
	23		do	do	DR SANDFORD RETD to DUTY
	24		do	do	No Casualties
	25		do	do	do
	26		do	do	do
	27		do	do	do
	28		do	do	do
	29		do	do	DR MORLEY RETD to DUTY
	30		do	do	do
	31		do	do	do

Army Form C. 2118

WAR DIARY
or
INTELLIGENCE SUMMARY
(Erase heading not required.)

Instructions regarding War Diaries and Intelligence Summaries are contained in F.S. Regs., Part II. and the Staff Manual respectively. Title Pages will be prepared in manuscript.

Place	Date	Hour	Summary of Events and Information	Remarks and references to Appendices
LA CRECHE	Aug 1	5-0 - 6-0 am 11.30 - 12.30 pm 4.0 - 5.15 pm	General Routine. Stables. Loading at Station by Supply Section. 7 am - Unloading at refilling point & refilling at 9.15 am wagons then proceeded to unite Baggage Section as detailed for general work.	APP
"	2		Usual routine. Very hot. G.O.C. Division inspected camp. T2/SR/01447 SSM COOK J. admitted T/36230 DR MORLEY W.H. 4/32 R Field Amb.	APP
"	3		Usual routine. Very hot.	APP
"	4		Usual routine. Very hot.	APP
"	5		Usual routine. Cooler. Visited Brigade HQrs. Usual routine. Fine. Visited 1st line transport of 2/1st K.R.R. 26th Royal Fusiliers, 10th R/y West Kent T/36230 DR MORLEY W.H. returned to duty.	APP
"	6		Usual routine. Very hot. Received 202 mules in exchange for sick H.D. horses. T2/SR/01447 SSM COOK J returned to duty.	APP

Army Form C. 2118

WAR DIARY
or
INTELLIGENCE SUMMARY
(Erase heading not required.)

Instructions regarding War Diaries and Intelligence Summaries are contained in F.S. Regs., Part II. and the Staff Manual respectively. Title Pages will be prepared in manuscript.

Place	Date	Hour	Summary of Events and Information	Remarks and references to Appendices
LA CRECHE	7		Usual Routine. Fine	R.P.R.
"	8		Usual Routine. Fine	RMR
"	9		Usual Routine. Hot.	RMR
"	10		Usual Routine. Hot.	RMR
"	11		Usual Routine. Hot.	RMR Left Coy 4th 14th Aust
"	12		Usual Routine. Hot.	RMR
"	13		Usual Routine. Fine	T3/027001 Dr SCALLY J admitted 10th Field Amb. RMR Recd.
"	14		Usual Routine. Stormy. The King passed whilst refilling was proceeding	T3/027001 DR SCALLY J returned to duty. RMR T5/7619 WHR DR RALEIGH J admitted 13th Field Amb. RMR C

1375 Wt. W593/826 1,000,000 4/15 J.B.C. & A. A.D.S.S./Forms/C. 2118.

Army Form C. 2118

WAR DIARY
or
INTELLIGENCE SUMMARY
(Erase heading not required.)

Instructions regarding War Diaries and Intelligence Summaries are contained in F.S. Regs., Part II. and the Staff Manual respectively. Title Pages will be prepared in manuscript.

Place	Date	Hour	Summary of Events and Information	Remarks and references to Appendices
LA CRECHE	Aug 15.		Usual Routine. Stormy. Visited Brigade H.Qs 322 Rfy Fusiliers, Machine Gun Coy.	APR.
"	16		Usual Routine. Stormy	RMR
"	17		Moved billets to LES TROIS TILLEULS, OUTERSTEEN. Refilled en route. Stormy. Visited Brigade H.Qs.	RMR
LES TROIS FERMES OUTERSTEEN	18.		Filled from depot & station at CAESTRE refilled at STRAZEELE. Stormy	RMR
"	19		Usual routine refilled at METEREN Stormy. Visited 140th Field Ambulance	RMR
"	20		Usual routine. Stormy. Visited 44th Field Ambulance 10th Queens.	RMR
"	21		Filled at CAESTRE at 9.8 am refilled at 12 noon. Fine	RMR
"	22		Filled at CAESTRE at 5.30am refilled at 8am paraded at billets 3 am left billets at 11pm to advance at BAILLEUL WEST. Fine.	RMR

Army Form C. 2118

WAR DIARY
or
INTELLIGENCE SUMMARY
(Erase heading not required.)

Instructions regarding War Diaries and Intelligence Summaries are contained in F.S. Regs., Part II. and the Staff Manual respectively. Title Pages will be prepared in manuscript.

Place	Date	Hour	Summary of Events and Information	Remarks and references to Appendices
LONG	23	12.30 p.m.	Began entraining at BAILLEUL WEST. Left Station 3.30 AM arrived PONT REMY 12.30 PM detrained & proceeded to LONG arriving 4 p.m. No casualties. Encamped on common. Fine, light rain in evening.	RMR
"	24		Repaired on ABBEVILLE - AILLY road south of BELLANCOURT. Visited all Infantry Brigade units. 10th Divn 26.02 Rly Fusiliers Fme. 21 KRR. Machine Gun Coy. Fine.	RMR
"	25		Usual Routine. STORMY	RMR
"	26		Usual Routine. Stormy. 7/026673 DR BEEVERS F/140 7/35561 DR BUCK E.E. Field Ambulance. adm to O.C. reinforcements BASE DEPOT LE HAVRE	RMR
"	27		Usual Routine. Stormy	RMR
"	28		Usual Routine. Stormy T/65/482 DR STOTT H. admitted to 140 FF Field Ambulance	RMR
"	29		Usual Routine. Thunderstorm. T/35555 DR FORD C.W. admitted to 138 FA Field Ambulance	RMR
"	30		Usual Routine. Very Wet. 7/026673 DR BEEVERS F. returned to duty	RMR
"	31		Usual Routine. Fine. T/65/482 DR STOTT H. returned to duty	RMR

Army Form C. 2118

WAR DIARY
or
INTELLIGENCE SUMMARY
(Erase heading not required.)

4 Coy 41st Div. Train

Instructions regarding War Diaries and Intelligence Summaries are contained in F.S. Regs., Part II. and the Staff Manual respectively. Title Pages will be prepared in manuscript.

Place	Date	Hour	Summary of Events and Information	Remarks and references to Appendices
	SEPT.			
LONG	1		Usual Stables 5 AM - 6 AM Routine 11.30 AM - 12.30 PM 4 P - 5.15 PM. Refilling 9.30 AM. General Supply Baggage road.	RM
"	2		Refilled on AILLY - ABBEVILLE road east cross roads PORT REMY - BUIGNY L'ABBE Fine T/36555 Dr FORD C.V. returned to duty	RM
"	3		Usual Routine Fine + Thunder storm	RM
"	4		Usual Routine Wet.	RM
"	5		Usual Routine with extra refill at 3.30 pm. Wet.	RM
"	6		Usual Routine Stormy	RM
"	7		Left LONG + trekked to ST SAUVEUR. No refill Fine	RM
ST SAUVEUR	7		Trecked to Mgf 62 D - D30 B4-1 near BUIRE refilled en route at 8pm Fine	RM

Army Form C. 2118

WAR DIARY
or
INTELLIGENCE SUMMARY
(Erase heading not required.)

HCoy. 41st Div¹ Train.

Place	Date	Hour	Summary of Events and Information	Remarks and references to Appendices
BUIRE	Sept 8.		Usual Routine. Fine.	RM
	9		Usual Routine. Fine.	RM
	10		Usual Routine. Fine. T/4079 CPL BAXTER C. returned to duty. No reft in order to drop cabin day ration hole.	RMR
	11		Supply Section refilled as usual. Coy moved to 62 D.E. 10 B	RMR
1 MILE SOUTH OF ALBERT	12		Refilling discontinued. 1st line transport drawing supplies from FRICOURT Stn. Fine. T/H/060712 Dr SEARS admitted to no 2 Field Ambulance	RMR
"	13		Coy Wagons on fatigue work. Stormy.	RMR
"	14		Fatigue work.	RMR
"	15		All baggage wagons rd to made all supply. No hot wind traps recommenced refilling with train supply wagon. Cold but fine.	RMR
"			Routine as above. Fine	RMR

1875 Wt. W593/826 1,000,000 4/15 J.B.C. & A. A.D.S.S./Forms/C. 2118.

WAR DIARY or **INTELLIGENCE SUMMARY**
(Erase heading not required.)

Army Form C. 2118

4 Coy 41st Divl Train

Place	Date	Hour	Summary of Events and Information	Remarks and references to Appendices
1 MILE STH OF ALBERT	Sept 16/16		Usual Routine. Fine. Surrounding camps shelled	RMR
"	17		Usual Routine. Refilled at MONTAUBAN. Fine	RMR
"	18		Usual Routine. Refilled on road by Camp. Moved back to old camp at BUIRE. Very Wet.	RMR
BUIRE L2D/D30 D4.1	19		Usual Routine. Refilled on BUIRE – DERNANCOURT road by Camp. Visited Bde HQs. WET.	RMR
"	20		Usual Routine. Stormy. T2/SR/01447 S.S.M. COOK A.T. admitted 140th Field Ambulance S4/070398 Pte BARBER C.H.M. admitted 140 Field Ambulance	RMR
"	21		Usual Routine. Stormy	RMR
"	22		Usual Routine. Fine. Visited all Bde units. Baggage wagons sent to units.	RMR
"	23		Usual Routine. Fine.	RMR
"	24		Usual Routine. Fine. Visited all Bde units.	RMR

Army Form C. 2118

WAR DIARY
or
INTELLIGENCE SUMMARY
(Erase heading not required.)

U Coy W127 D vl Tran.

Instructions regarding War Diaries and Intelligence Summaries are contained in F.S. Regs., Part II. and the Staff Manual respectively. Title Pages will be prepared in manuscript.

Place	Date SEPT	Hour	Summary of Events and Information	Remarks and references to Appendices
BUIRE 62D/R30/B4.1	25		Usual Routine Fine	RMR
	26		Usual Routine Fine	RMR
	27		Usual Routine Thunder Storm	RMR
	28		Usual Routine Stormy	RMR
	29		Usual Routine Wet. Baggage wagon returned to unit as no more required.	54/070398 PTE BARBER C.H.M. returned to duty. RMR
	30		Usual Routine Fine	D.C.Richn Capt. RMR

Army Form C. 2118

WAR DIARY
or
INTELLIGENCE SUMMARY
(Erase heading not required.)

4 Co, 4th Div / Train ML

Instructions regarding War Diaries and Intelligence Summaries are contained in F.S. Regs., Part II. and the Staff Manual respectively. Title Pages will be prepared in manuscript.

Place	Date	Hour	Summary of Events and Information	Remarks and references to Appendices
BUIRE	Oct. 1		Usual Routine = Stables 5.30–6.30 am. Refilling. Fatigues.	app
BÉCORDEL			Usual Routine, Baggage wagon to units. 11.0–12.0 Fine. 4.0–5.15.	app
BÉCORDEL	2		Refilled at BUIRE. Tricked to BÉCORDEL. Wet.	app
"	3		do BÉCORDEL Wet.	app.
"	4		Usual Routine. Baggage wagons returned from units. Wet.	app
"	5		Usual Routine. Stormy	app
"	6		Usual Routine. Fine	app
"	7		Filled at ALBERT 6.30 AM refilled BECORDEL Fine	app.

Army Form C. 2118

WAR DIARY
or
INTELLIGENCE SUMMARY
(Erase heading not required.)

Instructions regarding War Diaries and Intelligence Summaries are contained in F. S. Regs., Part II. and the Staff Manual respectively. Title Pages will be prepared in manuscript.

Place	Date Oct	Hour	Summary of Events and Information	Remarks and references to Appendices
BECORDEL	8		Usual Routine Wet Visited Bde HQs + units T/094277 Pt Harvey L admitted 140th Field Ambulance	
	9		Usual Routine Fine T/094209 Pt Harvey L returned to duty	
	10		Usual Routine Fine	
	11		Usual Routine Fine	
	12		Usual Routine Fine Visited Bde HQs & Units.	
	13		Filled at ALBERT refilled at BUIRE	
			Moved Camp to BUIRE Fine	
BUIRE	14		Filled at EDGEHILL refilled at BUIRE Fine	
	15		do Fine	
	16		Trekked to ARGOEUVES, refilled for Transport. Infantry trained to AIRAINES + refilled from motor lorries Fine	

WAR DIARY
or
INTELLIGENCE SUMMARY
(Erase heading not required.)

Army Form C. 2118

Instructions regarding War Diaries and Intelligence Summaries are contained in F.S. Regs., Part II. and the Staff Manual respectively. Title Pages will be prepared in manuscript.

Place	Date	Hour	Summary of Events and Information	Remarks and references to Appendices
	Oct			
ARGOEUVES	17		Trekked to AIRAINES and 6.45 then refilled. Fine	
AIRAINES	18		Refilled outside town Fine Stormy	
do	19		No refill. Entrained at LONGPRÉ at 6.21 PM	
Caistre	20		Detrained 6.10 am. Refill between Road 2 p.m. Stormy T/4 059720 S. Stanley E Admitted no 5 Stationary Hospital sec B Athwell Arrived Pinkroom 8.30 a.m. T/4 059720 S Stanley Returned to duty	Appx. Appx.
Pinkroom	21		Trekked to Renninghelst 9 a.m. arrived noon Fine	Appx.
Renninghelst	22		Refilled at Dress from Railhead 9 a.m. Wet	Appx.
Renninghelst	23		Drew from Railhead 8.15 a.m. Refilled 2 p.m. Fine	Appx.
Renninghelst	24		Weather Railhead 8.15 a.m. Wet Refilled	Appx.
Renninghelst	25		Drew from Railhead 7.45 — Refilled 11 a.m.	Appx.
Renninghelst	26		Drew from Railhead 7.45 — Stormy Refilled 11 a.m.	Appx.
Renninghelst	27		Drew from Railhead 7.45 a.m. Fine Wet Refilled 11 a.m. T/53119 Pte Butcher W.A. Admitted 140 Field Ambulance	Appx.

Army Form C. 2118

WAR DIARY
or
INTELLIGENCE SUMMARY
(Erase heading not required.)

Instructions regarding War Diaries and Intelligence Summaries are contained in F.S. Regs., Part II. and the Staff Manual respectively. Title Pages will be prepared in manuscript.

Place	Date	Hour	Summary of Events and Information	Remarks and references to Appendices
Rumghilat	28		Drew from Ration 7.45 — Refilled 11 a.m. Wet.	Appx
Rumghilat	29		Drew from Ration 7.45 — Refilled 11 a.m. Wet.	Appx
Rumghilat	30		Drew from Ration 7.45 — Refilled 11 a.m. Wet. 846/0717 Pte Bradshaw H admitted 140th Field Ambulance	Appx
Rumghilat	31		Drew from Ration 7.45 — Refilled 11 a.m. Wet.	Appx

Actg. O.C. 4 Coy.
141st Div. Train — 405
31 October 1916.

Army Form C. 2118

WAR DIARY
or
INTELLIGENCE SUMMARY
(Erase heading not required.)

No 4 Coy 1st Train
1st Pul Train

Place	Date	Hour	Summary of Events and Information	Remarks and references to Appendices
REMING-HELST G 34	Nov. 1		Usual Routine = Stables 6-7 11-12.15 3.30-4.45 Refilling by 1st Divl Transport.	Falling at WIPPENHOEK 7.50 Various transport fatigues.
	2		Usual Routine. Wet.	
	3		Usual Routine Wet.	54/070792 Pte BRADBURY.H. returned to duty
	4		Usual Routine Wet.	
	5		Usual Routine Fine	54/070792 T5/7608 WR D? PROCTOR admitted 140 Field Ambulance
	6		Usual Routine Wet.	T/31325 a/s S.S. NOLAN C. admitted 140 Field Ambulance
	7		Usual Routine Wet.	

Army Form C. 2118

Instructions regarding War Diaries and Intelligence Summaries are contained in F. S. Regs., Part II. and the Staff Manual respectively. Title Pages will be prepared in manuscript.

WAR DIARY
or
INTELLIGENCE SUMMARY
(Erase heading not required.)

Place	Date	Hour	Summary of Events and Information	Remarks and references to Appendices
REMING-HELST G.34	Nov 16		Coy. struck off usual duties for drills, inspections (foot) Route march all day. Fine frosty.	Copy
	17		Usual Routine. Fine frosty	
	18		do snow rain	
	19		do fine	
	20		do fine	
	21		Refilled in station yard & delivered rations to units fine	T4/058102 Dr BUTCHER W.H. admitted No 7 Field Amb. as sc.
	22		do fine	
	23		do fine	
	24		do fine	
			Visited 21st K.R.R. 26th R.T.	
	25		Visited Bde H.Q. 10th Queens 72 R.T. WH	RJP Edur

1875 Wt. W593/826 1,000,000 4/15 J.B.C. & A. A.D.S.S./Forms/C. 2118.

WAR DIARY
or
INTELLIGENCE SUMMARY

(Erase heading not required.)

Army Form C. 2118

Instructions regarding War Diaries and Intelligence Summaries are contained in F. S. Regs., Part II. and the Staff Manual respectively. Title Pages will be prepared in manuscript.

Place	Date	Hour	Summary of Events and Information	Remarks and references to Appendices
RENING-HEIST G 34	Nov 26		Usual Routine Fine	P of R of Cty.
	27		do Fine.	
	28		do Fine	
	29		do Fine	
	30		do Fine	

Army Form C. 2118

WAR DIARY
or
INTELLIGENCE SUMMARY
(Erase heading not required.)

Instructions regarding War Diaries and Intelligence Summaries are contained in F. S. Regs., Part II. and the Staff Manual respectively. Title Pages will be prepared in manuscript.

Place	Date	Hour	Summary of Events and Information	Remarks and references to Appendices
RENING-HELST G 34	Nov 8		Usual Routine. Wet	Copy
	9		Usual Routine. Fine	TS 7608 WHDR PROCTOR T.A. returned to duty.
	10		Usual Routine. Fine	
	11		Usual Routine. Fine Visited Bde HQs 10th R.W. Surrey Regt.	T4/057809 D: BUTCHER, W.H. returned to duty.
	12		Usual Routine. Fine	
	13		Usual Routine. Fine Visited 21st KRRs 26th ROYAL FUSILIERS	
	14		Usual Routine. Fine	
	15		Usual Routine. Fine	

Army Form C. 2118

WAR DIARY
or
INTELLIGENCE SUMMARY
(Erase heading not required.)

Instructions regarding War Diaries and Intelligence Summaries are contained in F. S. Regs., Part II. and the Staff Manual respectively. Title Pages will be prepared in manuscript.

Place	Date Dec	Hour	Summary of Events and Information	Remarks and references to Appendices
REMING-HELST	1		Usual Routine Stables 6 - 7 11 - 12 3.30 - 4.30.	Filling & Refilling at WIPPENHOEK at 6.30 am. (Horseman Ltt. for Riddlesmen Ltt. attached)
	2		Various Fatigues	
	3		Usual Routine	
	4		do	Fine
	5		do	do
	6		do	do
	7		do	do
	8		do	do
			do	Wet
			do	Fine
			do	Wet

WAR DIARY
or
INTELLIGENCE SUMMARY
(Erase heading not required.)

Army Form C. 2118

Place	Date	Hour	Summary of Events and Information	Remarks and references to Appendices
Ringfield	Dec 9th		Moved from line	
—	10th		do	Fine
—	11th		do	Fine
—	12th		do	Landing footg. Capt EP Richmond whilst walking on a football field – tripped, slipped & fractured his right leg in two places. He was admitted to No 140 Fd. F.A. T/17/125 Dr Liddle keyed SFd. Transferred No 3 Cap T/02/909 Dr Watson PM admitted No 6 FA. wire Loft. T4/05/107 Dr Butcher MA transferred from No 2 Cap 41 at first Train. T4/102/970 Dr Stewart A.C. to No 2 Cap 41 or front train Lieut L S Ladd acting OC Cap	R Richmond Capt T Liddle Capt Watson Lt. (sick)
	13		Moved from line	Rainy
	14th		do	do
	15th		do	Rainy Wet	Capt GH Colgraw Transferred Hup Cap Fd to No 2 Cap & to the OC Cap

WAR DIARY
or
INTELLIGENCE SUMMARY
(Erase heading not required.)

Army Form C. 2118

Place	Date	Hour	Summary of Events and Information	Remarks and references to Appendices
Henley-[?]	Dec 16th	—	Moved into line. Fine	C[?]
	17th	—	" "	C[?]
	18th	—	" "	C[?]
	19th	—	" " T4/234621 St Vincent J. transferred from res.	C[?]
	20th	—	" " 1 Coy w/ rations to Zon.	C[?]
	21st	—	Showery T5/01673 Dr Beaumont to no 1 Cy	C[?]
	22nd	—	" " T3/027091 Dr Watson transferred to duty	C[?]
	23rd	—	Stormy	C[?]
	24th	—	Stormy T5/027091 Dr Watson not transferred to	C[?]
	25th	—	" " no 1 Cy A.	C[?]
	26th	—	Windy	C[?]
	27th	—	Rain	C[?]
	28th	—	Rain	C[?]
	29th	—	Windy & Rain	C[?]

Army Form C. 2118

WAR DIARY
or
INTELLIGENCE SUMMARY
(Erase heading not required.)

Place	Date	Hour	Summary of Events and Information	Remarks and references to Appendices
[illegible]	30th		[illegible] Showery	(*c*
	31st		[illegible]	(*c*
				(* Telegram rept'd No 4 Company 41st Regiment Train

WAR DIARY
or
INTELLIGENCE SUMMARY

(Erase heading not required.)

Army Form C. 2118

Instructions regarding War Diaries and Intelligence Summaries are contained in F.S. Regs., Part II. and the Staff Manual respectively. Title Pages will be prepared in manuscript.

Place	Date	Hour	Summary of Events and Information	Remarks and references to Appendices
RENINGHELST	1/7		About 11 a.m. Arthur Fair S/6457.70 off eye right shoulder hit entry left.	C.A.C
—	2/7		From Fair	C.A.C
—	3/7		From Fair	C.A.C
—	4/7		M.R. & Army	C.A.C
—	5/7		From Bull	C.A.C
—	6/7		No 74/082033 Dr Lowe J. Ledder slightly admitted to 7th F.A. suffering from Shell wound and burned at YPRES.	C.A.C
—	7/7		From Army Pkin	C.A.C
—	8/7		No 74/06033 Dr Lowe J, No 74/06587 Dr Wilder L Earp Fg, wounded acid.	C.A.C

WAR DIARY
or
INTELLIGENCE SUMMARY
(Erase heading not required.)

Army Form C. 2118

Instructions regarding War Diaries and Intelligence Summaries are contained in F. S. Regs., Part II. and the Staff Manual respectively. Title Pages will be prepared in manuscript.

Place	Date	Hour	Summary of Events and Information	Remarks and references to Appendices
Rennykhel	9/7		Fine. Horse-lines, my tents, camp site inspected by 2nd Army Inoculation &c., & found satisfactory.	(A+C
	10/7		Showery	(A+C
	11/7		Still	(A+C
	12/7		Showery	(A+C
	13/7		Stormy	(A+C
	14/7		Fine & dry. no TISR/199 Lt Ellis N admitted 132nd F.A.	(A+C
	15/7		Fine & dry	(A+C
	16/7		Showery	(A+C
	17/7		Fine & dry. Inc. of Artillery for dry allotted to 10-30 am	(A+C
	18/7		Fine & dry	(A+C
	19/7		Fine & dry	(A+C
	20/7		Fine & dry. Time of reveillie by Bug changed to 8 am. Useful Draft of 308 half & other Reserve Army Field Hospits to strings war & roads N.W. of Helen outs in of Ren Kennel turned of foot.	(A+C
	21/7			(A+C

Army Form C. 2118

WAR DIARY
or
INTELLIGENCE SUMMARY
(Erase heading not required.)

Instructions regarding War Diaries and Intelligence Summaries are contained in F.S. Regs., Part II. and the Staff Manual respectively. Title Pages will be prepared in manuscript.

Place	Date	Hour	Summary of Events and Information	Remarks and references to Appendices
RENINGHELST	21/7		An Enreid T4/20/598 St John H.B. Transferred from 23 H.T.S. short T.1.S.R./0239.6 to Keen L. do do do T4/20/598 do Jno H.B. Transferred 15.140 to #A do T1.S.R./0239.6 to Keen L. do do do	CMC
	22/7	Menal Newton Trinity	T4/12417 St Dembery granted leave of absence to U.K. 22 July to 1 2/17 An active rifle gr. 1, days supplies of horse & oats to Brigade was made, sent the stan & ammunition under 21/7. T1.S.R./179 St Ellis W. discharged hospital wounded dated 21/7, notified 23/7	CMC
	23/7	do	do	CMC
	24/7	do	do	CMC
	25/7	do	do	CMC
	26/7	do	do	CMC
	27/7	do	Supply train arrived Westoutre berk 1-45 hrs refilling pt. take on convoy 2 mes. T4/057947 6 Cpl/c dvr Riley P.J. transferred to new Army H.Q. 1st ord. Train T1.S.R./01140 Cpl. Wolpole J. appointed a/c dvr Cpl. O. Clerry, Batteller 16/10/17. Supply Train arrived 4-30 hrs	CMC

WAR DIARY
or
INTELLIGENCE SUMMARY
(Erase heading not required.)

Army Form C. 2118

Instructions regarding War Diaries and Intelligence Summaries are contained in F.S. Regs., Part II. and the Staff Manual respectively. Title Pages will be prepared in manuscript.

Place	Date	Hour	Summary of Events and Information	Remarks and references to Appendices
RENINGHELST	28/7		Usual Routine. Frosty	(A/C
	29/7		do. do. Conference	(A/C
	30/7		do. do and Slight Snow. Tank, horses etc inspected	(A/C
	31/7		do. by O.C. 41st Bn. Train. Slight thaw after long continued frost.	(A/C
				(Telegram kept O.C. 4 Bty 4/ at Div'l Train

WAR DIARY
or
INTELLIGENCE SUMMARY
(Erase heading not required.)

Army Form C. 2118

Place	Date	Hour	Summary of Events and Information	Remarks and references to Appendices
Reninghelst	1/7/17		Usual routine. Refilled at Watphenloek 8 am Brsty.	C+C
"	2/7/17		" " " " " Brsty.	C+C
"	3/7/17		" " Train arrived 12.45. BN	M.P.
"	4/7/17		" " " " 1.10 pm	M.P.
"	5/7/17		" " " " "	M.P.
"	6/7/17		" " TS/8697 Saddler Sergt Artun D appointed Q/saddler Staff Sergt	M.P.
"	7/7/17		" " " "	M.P.
"	8/7/17		" " " "	M.P.
"	9/7/17		" " T2SR/03773 Dr Hood A.S.C. transferred from 52nd M.S. Vet to this Company	M.P.
"	10/7/17		" " Train arrived 2.45 pm	M.P.
"	11/7/17		" " " "	M.P.
"	12/7/17		" " Thawing	M.P.
"	13/7/17		" " TS/7619 Wheeler Raleigh.T was admitted to 138th Field Ambulance	M.P.
"	14/7/17		" " S4/070722 A/Cpl Satterthwaite.D transferred from No 2 Coy 4th Divisional Train to this Company	M.P.
"	15/2/17		" " Brsty.	M.P.
"	16/2/17		" " Thawing	M.P.
"	17/2/17		" " Thawing Thaw has been in force from midnight 16th inst.	C+C
"	18/2/17		" " Thaw day	C+C

Army Form C. 2118

WAR DIARY
or
INTELLIGENCE SUMMARY
(Erase heading not required.)

Instructions regarding War Diaries and Intelligence Summaries are contained in F.S. Regs., Part II. and the Staff Manual respectively. Title Pages will be prepared in manuscript.

Place	Date	Hour	Summary of Events and Information	Remarks and references to Appendices
Reninghelst	19/2/17	Noonish	Rain ... Thawing	
"	20/2/17	do	Raw	Two of Belling & Wishen had altered to 10-30 fine. [illegible] Raleigh returned to duty from 140 & Field Ambulance	
"	21/2/17	do	Foggy		
"	22/2/17	do	Rain		
"	23/2/17	do	Dull	[illegible] Saddlers Series Roble How transferred from BHJD to 4 Bty #1 did Trains T/36694 Dr Hayes. Transferred from AHTO & Bty to 140 at SA T/030.94 Dr Wright	
"	24/2/17	do	Fair		
"	25/2/17	do	Dull		
"	26/2/17	do	Fine		
"	27/2/17	do	Fine	Thaw set in about midnight	
"	28/2/17	do	Frost		

(sd) [illegible] Capt.
O.C. 4 Bty 41 [illegible] Train

Army Form C. 2118

WAR DIARY
or
INTELLIGENCE SUMMARY
(Erase heading not required.)

Instructions regarding War Diaries and Intelligence Summaries are contained in F.S. Regs., Part II. and the Staff Manual respectively. Title Pages will be prepared in manuscript.

Place	Date	Hour	Summary of Events and Information	Weather	Remarks and references to Appendices
RENINGHELST	1/7		Moved here from Reninghelst 10-30 am 7/18518 Lieut Sgt Vesper transferred from SOS 9/12 Pte Jones E transferred from 1/5 to 2nd South Stafford Regt S4/058766 Pte Knox G transferred from 4/6 to 41st Divisional HQ 75/6365 Farrier Staff Whiting R. Wakington transferred to CCS 14 de F.A.	Fine	(MC
	2/7		"	Dull Frosty	(MC
	3/7		"	Frosty Snow	(MC
	4/7		"	Frost	(MC
	5/7		"	Frosty Snow	(MC
	6/7		"	Frosty Dull	(MC
	7/7		"	Fine	(MC
	8/7		"		(MC
	9/7		"		(MC
	10/7		"		
	11/7		"		

Army Form C. 2118

WAR DIARY
or
INTELLIGENCE SUMMARY
(Erase heading not required.)

Instructions regarding War Diaries and Intelligence Summaries are contained in F.S. Regs., Part II. and the Staff Manual respectively. Title Pages will be prepared in manuscript.

Place	Date	Hour	Summary of Events and Information	Remarks and references to Appendices
RENINGHELST	12/3/15		Naval Howitzer	(A.C.
	13/3/15		do Firing	(A.C.
	14/3/15		do Idle	(A.C.
	15/3/15		do Showing	(A.C.
	16/3/15		do Firing	(A.C.
	17/3/15		do Firing 1 HO hy no 56 destroyed	(A.C.
	18/3/15		do Firing	(A.C.
	19/3/15		do do	(A.C.
	20/3/15		do do	(A.C.
			do do	
	21/3/15		Same Hqrs of *billing changed to 8 am Bygly & bungof fought this unit for 12 MO Batchmally to good area. T4/057226 Dr Turner G.S. } from 13HTD to T4/093276 Dr Brown G.S. } no 4 hy 41 siege T4/186194 Dr Patterson s/J } Bty Brown T4/057245 Dr Lumley s/J } From Hy to T4/093276 Dr Brown S/M } 140 at F.A. T4/106194 Dr Patterson s/J } attached to Supply Wagon 124 R.G.Hy units for one 10 of 2 others hy for one 21.o.t KRR	(A.C.

WAR DIARY
or
INTELLIGENCE SUMMARY

(Erase heading not required.)

Army Form C. 2118

Place	Date	Hour	Summary of Events and Information	Remarks and references to Appendices
STEENVOORDE	22/7/17		Moved from tws [illegible] 11th Bgde not over, refilling as usual at Watten [?]	(A/c
	23/7/17		Stormy Begg. wagon reported lay	(A/c
	24/7/17		Fine	(A/c
	25/7/17		Fine	(A/c
	26/7/17		Rain T/o 57482 Pt Scott A.H. admitted to 139 L.F.A. had been late refilling 12.45	(A/c
	27/7/17		Fair Refilling 1-30 am as up to had been being shots.	(A/c
	28/7/17		Fine Tar/late refilling at 2-20 pm T4/129508 Pt Smith C from DH T.D.S. T4/129508 " dit Pt 140 & F.A.	(A/c
	29th		Showery Refilling at 10 am, the H.D destroyed.	(A/c
	30th		Fair	(A/c
	31st		Fine Cpl. W. Entwistle O.C.H. lay. 41st Brit Div.	(A/c

Army Form C. 2118

WAR DIARY
or
INTELLIGENCE SUMMARY
(Erase heading not required.)

Place	Date	Hour	Summary of Events and Information	Remarks and references to Appendices
Steenvoorde	1/7		Usual Routine	
	2/7		do	
	3/7		do	
	4/7		do	
	5/7		do	
	6/7		do	
Reninghelst	7/7		do	

WAR DIARY
or
INTELLIGENCE SUMMARY

Army Form C. 2118

Place	Date	Hour	Summary of Events and Information	Remarks and references to Appendices
RENINGHELST	7/7		Normal Routine	
	8/7		Fine	C in C
	9/7		Showery S/41626497 L/Cpl Boyle E.H. appointed unpaid L/Cpl w.e.f 3/4/3/7 wich effect from 1/7. T/4/07017 Acf L/Cpl Scott R.D returned to duty. Gnr D.R.W.S. T/4/058590 Dr Barry JW admitted 130 F.A.	C in C
	10/7		Still Fine do do returned to duty.	C in C
	11/7		Fine	C in C
	12/7		Windy Fine "	C in C
	13/7		" All Ranks in trenches in area of Bac Rochinkim & Halnuts Gap P.H. by Sg Gds recd. T/4/058590 Dr Barry JW admitted 139 F.A.	C in C
	14/7		Showery T/3/06059 Dr W Boyle J. returned to duty.	C in C
	15/7		Fine T/4/058590 Dr Barry JW returned to duty.	C in C
	16/7		"	C in C
	17/7		Snow & Rain	C in C
	18/7		Spraying T/4/13852 Dr Sinclair J. to No 2 hvy 4/st But team	C in C
	19/7		Showery T/113394 Dr Winslow S. from No 2 hvy	C in C

WAR DIARY or INTELLIGENCE SUMMARY

Army Form C. 2118

(Erase heading not required.)

Place	Date	Hour	Summary of Events and Information	Remarks and references to Appendices
RENINGHELST	20/4/17	Noon	Hard shelling at Micken Hoek changed to 10-15 A.M., shelling taking about an hour approximately.	CRE
			No. T4/020721 Dvr Lyle sent S.O. owing to permanent grade of own being unsuitable to establish habit, his conduct went satisfactory while sobering being here.	
	21/4/17	do	T4/058590 Sjt Begg J.W. admitted 139th F.A. T4/058570 Dr Begg F. returned to duty T3/024471 Dr Jones F. transferable at from Base Depot (H.T.v.d.) T4/17.9944 Dr Warr transferred sick to 2nd Army H.Q.	CRE
	22/4/17	do		CRE
	23/4/17	do	Reck train came in very late. T/36452 Dr Hughes Cpl J to 140th F.A. T4/065793 Dr Rooney A admitted 138th F.A. who was wounded by an anti-aircraft shell. S Wagon S/Sjt Groff and men behind Gragn detailed for duty given less permanently (possibly) T4/05856 Dr. F. Trench Warfare School T.10 Corps CRE	CRE

1375 Wt. W593/826 1,000,000 4/15 J.B.C. & A. A.D.S.S./Forms/C. 2118.

WAR DIARY
or
INTELLIGENCE SUMMARY
(Erase heading not required.)

Army Form C. 2118

Place	Date	Hour	Summary of Events and Information	Remarks and references to Appendices
RENING HELST	24/8/17		Manal Ren Em Fine T.O.16529 3 St Row A wreaked to CES	(MC
	25/8/17		do do	(MC
	26/8/17		do do	(MC
	27/8/17		do Faint	(MC
	28/8/17		do Fine	(MC
	29/8/17		do Fine	Two monuments reviewed (HO) The enemy shelled on the vicinity of into last night from 3 pm to 5 pm invariably large shells, fell immediately to the north appearing to the east (no peaks away), apparently very little damage done.	(MC
	30/8/17		do Fine		(MC

Chalgrove Capt.
O.C. H Coy HOD Section

WAR DIARY
or
INTELLIGENCE SUMMARY
(Erase heading not required.)

Army Form C. 2118

Place	Date	Hour	Summary of Events and Information	Remarks and references to Appendices
RENINGHELST	1/5/17		Moved Rankers Farm	
	2/5/17		do	
	3/5/17		do	Artillery at Muffen hoek enemy at 10-15am too enemy of 30 of S/30/256 Rg Inged T Cart. Rd E from Baw Sept 14 T Lyst Tu/0/B 293 (pt Ravir) A returned to duty from 2nd CCS.	(MC
			do		(MC
			do	Two horses were dropped in the camp from hostile aircraft about 11-30 am. Three horses Rd be many? front? fails to detect.	(MC
	4/5/17		do		(MC
	5/5/17		do	Brig'd & Supply Wag'ns of 26th Bat'n RF? filled stores and moved to that area.	(MC
	6/5/17		do	Savy? formely to that area. Captain Culligan proceeded on leave to England. F/SR 01405 C.S.M Wigston.T } proceeded to 2nd Army T/o 26737 Pte. Saunders F } Rest Camp. F/SR 02198 Dr Howard W. }	N/P

WAR DIARY
or
INTELLIGENCE SUMMARY
(Erase heading not required.)

Army Form C. 2118

Instructions regarding War Diaries and Intelligence Summaries are contained in F.S. Regs., Part II. and the Staff Manual respectively. Title Pages will be prepared in manuscript.

Place	Date	Hour	Summary of Events and Information	Remarks and references to Appendices
RENINGHELST	7.5.17		Usual Routine. Fine	M.P.
	8.5.17		-do- Rain	M.P.
	9.5.17		-do- Fine	M.P.
	10.5.17		-do- Fine	M.P.
	11.5.17		-do- -do- T/4079 Cpl Baker granted leave to England. 10/5/17 to 20/5/17	M.P.
			1 Officer + 4 O.R. of 9 Corps Railhead Detachment, attached for rations & rations from 12/5/17	M.P.
	12.5.17		-do- Fine T3/026737 L/Cpl Sawdon F. transferred to No.2 Coy 41st Div Train DSC	M.P.
	13.5.17		-do- Showery T/36792 a/Cpl Kirk T. from No.2 Coy 41st Div Train A.S.C	M.P.
	14.5.17		-do- Fine	M.P.
	15.5.17		-do- Fine	M.P.
	16.5.17		-do- Fine. Baggage Wagons sent to Units	M.P.
NOORDPEENE	17.5.17		Rain 1 Officer 4 NCOs + Supply Section horses + drivers detached to R.E. at VLAMERTINGHE. Wagons left and No.2 Coy H.Q.Company moved out of Camp at 7.A.M, refilled at WIPPENHOEK en route. Arrived NOORDPEENE 6.30 P.M. T2SR/02863 Dr Huntin of No.1 Coy proceed to England on 8 days leave. 17.5.17 to 27.5.17	M.P.
SALPERWICK	18.5.17		Fine Moved off 7 A.M. arrived at SALPERWICK in the 124 Bde area at 11.30 A.M.	M.P.
	19.5.17		Fine Drew forage & rations for 19.5.17 at HOULLE at 9.30 A.M. Rations + forage delivered by motor lorries for consumption on 20th inst.	M.P.

1875 Wt. W593/826 1,000,000 4/15 J.B.C. & A. A.D.S.S./Forms/C.2118.

Army Form C. 2118

WAR DIARY
or
INTELLIGENCE SUMMARY
(Erase heading not required.)

Instructions regarding War Diaries and Intelligence Summaries are contained in F.S. Regs., Part II. and the Staff Manual respectively. Title Pages will be prepared in manuscript.

Place	Date	Hour	Summary of Events and Information	Remarks and references to Appendices
SALPERNICK	19.5.17 (cont'd)		Att (fine) Baggage horses returned + 4 wagons returned from Units	M.P.
	20.5.17		Fine. Forage + rations delivered by motor lorries. Company routine	M.P.
	21.5.17		Dull " "	M.P.
	22.5.17		Raining. Company routine	M.P.
	23.5.17		Fine. "	M.P.
	24.5.17		" "	M.P.
	25.5.17		" "	M.P.
			T4/060721 Dvr Scott S.D reinstated with appointment of A/Cpl 20.4.17 authority ASC Sect Adj Gen's office at the Base No 8/6213/6 17.5.17	M.P.
	26.5.17		Fine. Company routine. T4/060721 A/Cpl Scott S.D transferred to Base Depot above. Surplus to establishment.	M.P.
	27.5.17		Weather fine. Company routine.	M.P.
	28.5.17		" "	M.P.
	29.5.17		Fair. "	M.P.
	30.5.17		Fine "	M.P.
			T2/11241 Cpl Jnottings D killed by shell fire, also horse killed + saddle destroyed. T/11241 Cpl Jnottings turned position H. 3 C 22. Sheet 28. Dvr H.D. horses evacuated to 52" Mob Vet. Baggage wagons horses + drivers formed.	M.P.
	31.5.17		Fair. Company HQs moved off at 2oo to return to Divisional Area. Refilled en route at HATTEN. Arrived at NORDHEENE 6.30.	M.P.

M. Boult Lt Capt
O.C. No 4 Coy. 4 Div Train RSC

Army Form C. 2118

WAR DIARY
or
INTELLIGENCE SUMMARY
(Erase heading not required.)

Instructions regarding War Diaries and Intelligence Summaries are contained in F.S. Regs., Part II. and the Staff Manual respectively. Title Pages will be prepared in manuscript.

Place	Date	Hour	Summary of Events and Information	Remarks and references to Appendices
RENINGHELST	1-6-17		Fine. HQ or B Coy moved off from Proofheere at 6 AM, joining and 12th Brig. Transport. Arrived RENINGHELST at 5 PM. Supply Section refilled at OUDERDOM siding at 3 PM	W.D
	2.6.17		Supply Section rejoined Company. Camp reference 6.84 6.75 Mah. 28 N.W.	M.P.
			Fine. Refilled at 1 PM.	
	3.6.17		Fine. 74/05745T Dr Edenburg R.P. to train H.Q. 736038 Dr Nelson G. from train V.D.	M.P.
	4.6.17		Vacated camp at 6 PM. ?? to hold shelling. Returned to camp 8 PM.	
			Fine. Usual Routine. 74/05487 Dr Churchill WP.IV evacuated to C.C.S. gassed (slight)	M.P.
			9.30 AM to 10.30 AM enemy shelled vicinity of camp. Moved camp 3.5 PM arrived	M.P.
			in new camp. 3.20. Camp reference Sheet 28 N.W. M 3 c, 3.8.	M.P.
	5.6.17		Fine. Usual Routine. Refilled 8.30 AM	M.P.
	6.6.17		Fine. "	M.P.
	7.6.17		"	M.P.
	8.6.17		Thundery, unsettled. Usual Routine.	
	9.6.17		Fine. Usual Routine.	M.P.
	10.6.17		Fine. T. Filling at 10.30 am HQ to 66 evacuated to M.V.S. Shrapnel wounds	C.M.C
	11.6.17		Fine. " to "	C.M.C
			Fine. "	C.M.C
	12.6.17		Fine. received 1 H.O. from reinforcements. Moved camp to new refce of ?? 28 N.W. B 7.5.	C.M.C
	13.6.17		Fine. Violent thunderstorm about 2 AM in the morning	C.M.C
OUDERDOM	14.6.17		Fine. Moved camp at 9.15 am to new ?? of new refce 28 N.W. G 36 A 3.7.	C.M.C
	15.6.17		Fine. T. Filling at 8.15 am	C.M.C
	16.6.17		Fine. T. Filling at 7.10 am 736538 Dr Milner G. to hos. leg M. & Dr Lewis	C.M.C
			745404478 to duty of from M.V.S. of from arm leg M	C.M.C

WAR DIARY
or
INTELLIGENCE SUMMARY
(Erase heading not required.)

Army Form C. 2118

Place	Date	Hour	Summary of Events and Information	Remarks and references to Appendices
OUDERDOM	17/6/15		Rifling at attached Ouderdom at 9am Marched from Rifling at attached at 3am away to enemy Ouderdom trenches twenty rounds gunnery	CMC
	18/6/15		S/4/0599/71 aty gunnery Wks no 3 Coy S/Sgt 415 Pte Brown B.B. transferred from 2nd Hdqs. Weather unsettled. Violent thunderstorm	CMC
	19/6/15		Marched throughout with rain	CMC
			T/4/244330 Cpl Evans W from 2nd coy remained 6 twenty of Camp killed. Vacated camp & to be felled filling in trenches left without casualties, on orders received, returned in our lorr. travel camp 9pm to 2 MWE M4 C	CMC
NENINGHELSTHO	20/6/15		Showery	CMC
	21/6/15		T/for/go/71 Pte Patrick Lambert back transferred to Base Depot Havre (HTrS) surplus	CMC
	22/6/15		nile travel camp to G 34 C4 3.	CMC

WAR DIARY
or
INTELLIGENCE SUMMARY
(Erase heading not required.)

Army Form C. 2118

Place	Date	Hour	Summary of Events and Information	Remarks and references to Appendices
RENING HELST	23/6/17		Rifling to 3 AM at Mithertart. Weather fine. Moved camp at 1.15 pm to 28 NW M.4.c. T/30126 Sgt Mulvaney J. admitted 140th FA.	CMC
	24/6/17		T/11334 Pte Chafford W admitted 140th FA	CMC
	25/6/17		T/30126 Sgt Mulvaney J returned to duty	CMC CMC
	26/6/17		Fair	CMC
	27/6/17		do Rifling at 5.30 am throughout evening	CMC
	28/6/17		do Rain & afterwards fine T4/250123 Rfl Storey E from BHTO	CMC
	29/6/17		Rain & a very heavy thunderstorm in the evening. Fine. Bgd 92nd army dispatched to units for Brigade move to the Lavera.	CMC
	30/6/17		Weather very wet. Holge of lay moved to sheet 27 SE. X4A.8.9. 1 Fontaine Houdeby moved off from all camp at 7.45 am arrived in new area at 10.30 am Rfilling at 19 D 3.0, Dublin brought there by MT	CMC

Telegrams left etc.
I C 4 May 41, at Bu L'Avore

WAR DIARY
or
INTELLIGENCE SUMMARY

(Erase heading not required.)

Army Form C. 2118

Place	Date	Hour	Summary of Events and Information	Remarks and references to Appendices
FONTAINE HUICK	1/7/17		Refilling at METEREN of lo filling at LAESTRE at 11 am T/11334 Sr Elwell S evacuated to L 23 6 T/4/108249 Sr Saunders N admitted 140th F.A. Weather dull. Bagg & wagon reported by s/c Brennan more to John Elba.	C.A.C.
	2/7		Weather fair. Normal Routine	C.A.C.
	3/7		" Fine "	C.A.C.
	4/7		" Dull "	C.A.C.
	5/7		" Fine " T/3/27016 Sr Trotter S admitted 140th F.A.	C.A.C.
	6/7		" Fine "	C.A.C.
	7/7		" Fine "	C.A.C.
	8/7		" Wet "	C.A.C.
	9/7		" Dull "	C.A.C.
	10/7		" Fine " T/4/108249 Sr Saunders returned to Duty T/3/7608 Wheeler Sr Proctor admitted 140th F.A.	C.A.C.
	11/7		" Fine " Refilling at 11 AM at METEREN, filling at LAESTRE at 8·45 am	C.A.C.

WAR DIARY
or
INTELLIGENCE SUMMARY

Army Form C. 2118

Place	Date	Hour	Summary of Events and Information	Remarks and references to Appendices
FONTAINE HOUCK	12/7/15		Weather fine. Men resting	(AC)
	13/7/15		do	(AC)
	14/7/15		do T3/0707618 Pte Trotter R returned to duty	(AC)
	15/7/15		do T5/7608 Wheelwright Private J.A. returned to duty	(AC)
	16/7/15		do T4/057442 Pte Stott H admitted 14.0. of S.A.	(AC)
	17/7/15		do T4/057488 Pte Short A organized 2nd cc S	(AC)
Westoutre	18/7/15		do Baggage wagons joined units for Brigade move. Rifles to METEREN on preceding trip, H'qrs & Coy moved to WESTOUTRE white plate 28 SW J, MJ 3 c 2.2.	(AC)
	19/7/15		do No 2017580 Pte Worthington H of 238th Employment Coy attached this company, admitted 14.0 of J.A. Accidentally injured. Refilling at cafe JM 3.C.2.2. (Duffs convoy. Line of Supply column) at 1pm. Baggage wagons arrived from units. Supply train no 16 Lockton DAC & 107 as usual. Brigade formed for temporary attachment, whole unit being fully ab...	(AC)

Army Form C. 2118

WAR DIARY or INTELLIGENCE SUMMARY
(Erase heading not required.)

Place	Date	Hour	Summary of Events and Information	Remarks and references to Appendices
WESTOUTRE	20/7/17		Weather fine. Artillery at 12 midday. Supply Wgn. 190 for Arty Brigade joined the temporary detachment of A.A. unit for duty.	(wc)
	21/7/17	do	Lt B3 L McDonald from no 3 Coy T4/213869 Dr Saddler Metcalfe adjt from 8 Base Sept HTPS T4/232102 Dr Mountain W.J. T4/178590 Dr Metcalfe W.J. S/016383 Pte Lunberg W. admitted 140 d F.A.	(wc)
	22/7/17	do	Supply Wgn. Detacht BAC, 187 & 190 Artillery Bgds. returned 2865	(wc)
	23/7/17	do	T5/8383 Farrier the Mattar admitted 140 d F.A.	635 (wc)
	24/7/17	do	T4/213869 Dr Saddler Metcalfe returned to base, employed to watch for Army and T.Army returned same day Refitting at 80 & 5 AM BRULOOSE.	(wc)
RENINGHELST	25/7/17	Rain	14 O.R. reported to Slit 28 dvl M ??? 11.A.3.9. T5/8363 Sh? Farrier the Mattar returned to duty	(wc)
	26/7/17	fine		(wc)
	27/7/17	fine		(wc)
	28/7/17	do	S/016383 Private Lunberg W admitted to duty by M/r Loftus to H do duty 28/7/80	(wc)

WAR DIARY
or
INTELLIGENCE SUMMARY

(Erase heading not required.)

Army Form C. 2118

Instructions regarding War Diaries and Intelligence Summaries are contained in F. S. Regs., Part II. and the Staff Manual respectively. Title Pages will be prepared in manuscript.

Place	Date	Hour	Summary of Events and Information	Remarks and references to Appendices
RENINGHELST	29/7		Weather wet	C/we
	30/7		do Showery 74/1.65.300 1st Reserve E detachment to 130 "7A	C/we
	31/7		do Fine 2L Bde on arrival now joined to 3 Bdg	C/we

Chagnon Capt.
O.C. 4 Bdg 1st Brigade

Army Form C. 2118

WAR DIARY
or
INTELLIGENCE SUMMARY

(Erase heading not required.)

Place	Date	Hour	Summary of Events and Information	Remarks and references to Appendices
RENINGHELST	1/8/17		Wet. Rain all day. Filling at Boulogne at 8-45 am and refilling in camp. Ent. at 11 am	(MC
	2/8/17		do. Rain all day. Normal Routine. Establishment of drivers reduced from 12 to 9 under Army Reorganisation (Hind June H&p). T4/114112 Dr Bill that admitted No.1 F.A.	(MC
	3/8/17		do. Dr Bartlett (T4/141411) transferred to C.C.D.	(MC
	4/8/17		do. L/Wgn. I horse Killed by enemy shell "B" section (Remmer) MC 673/02 5684 Dr Emery from Base Depot Havre	(MC
			T4/221 854 do do	
			T4/221 845 do Lim th. AE as 14o of FA	
	5/8/17		Fine. 3 Wgn. & horse detailed for duty with 235 Field Coy RE.	(MC
	6/8/17		do. Bad. Reached at BAILLEUL Filling at 7-45 am T/140.86 Dr. Lockey go from Base Depot HAVRE.	(MC
	7/8/17		do. T/114086 do do as 140 of F.A.	(MC
	8/8/17		do. Filling at BAILLEUL at 8-45 am & detailed my use	(MC
	9/8/17		do. Lmg 197 date "D" withdrawn (Promoted attached to Lay)	(MC
	10/8/17		Fine. Waterloo Wgn returned from 235 Coy RE).	(MC

WAR DIARY
or
INTELLIGENCE SUMMARY
(Erase heading not required.)

Army Form C. 2118

Place	Date	Hour	Summary of Events and Information	Remarks and references to Appendices
RENINGHELST	11 8/17	Weather Dull	Filling at BRULOOZE at 9 AM	(AC
	12 8/17	Showery	W.Wagon TPgr dets led to 233 Lg R Engineers. 1st Class horses so q men busy till detachment. Wagons which failed to roll had to return, have short is very narrow time q wagons have replacements had auxiliates.	(AC
	13 8/17	Fair	Filling at BRULOOZE at 10 AM, refilling completed in same by 2 pm approx. Baggage Wagon dispatched to Maj. for Billoland dure. 2 Lt. S looked on for Journale on attachment to log.	(AC
	14 8/17	Fair	T4/05/8109 to Batches W.H. adm other 140 d J.A.	(AC
THIEUSHOUK	15 8/17	Rain	Filling at BAILLEUL at 9-30 AM Refilling at Q29.D.8.7. Half of log sent to dictts and out first at 1-30h T4/23/15 Lt Jordan Advy. Littu to 11th A.C.S. on HD Leave received for one day	(AC
	16 8/17	Fine		(AC
	17 8/17	Fine Fair	Hostile aircraft dropped bombs on camp at about 9-45 pm on 17/8/17, it fell in officers lines, and 2 nd Lt G Slaving OC ASC Officers billed as killed in small 2 nd Lt Sharkson	(AC
	18 8/17			(AC

WAR DIARY
or
INTELLIGENCE SUMMARY
(Erase heading not required.)

Army Form C. 2118

Place	Date	Hour	Summary of Events and Information	Remarks and references to Appendices
THIEUSHUK	18/8/17		Wards	
			Was not dealt by the am tank and admitted to 11 X X L others were no other wounded to Infantry units in area for minimity suffered. Fine. Refilling forward etc.	CWC
	19/8/17		2nd Lt. G. Manning too sick but met in to funnel in a field outside at Shel 27 S.E. Q 29. D. 99.	CWC
	20/8/17		Fine. Lilley Bailleul down time. Refilling at #18.C.8.1	CWC
	21/8/17		Fine. Filling 8am Bailleul Refilling 10am at 18 C.8.1.	CWC
	22/8/17		Fine. Nature Rubin	CWC
	23/8/17		Showing to filling at 8-30AM	CWC
	24/8/17		Unsettled. Owing to late arrival of Pack from filling at 1 am. Baggage wagons dispatched as usual for Brigade ends.	CWC
STAPLE	25/8/17		Fine	H.Q of Coy moved to STAPLE at 7AM. Refilling from #18th Divisional Supply Column at STAPLE fat 4 hm.	CWC
SCADERBOURG	6/9/17		Fine	H.Q of Coy moved to SCADERBOURG that 27 A SE R 33 A.B.4. Coy moved at 6am and arrived here at 10.45 AM. Refilling from Supply Column at 1 hm.	CWC

WAR DIARY
or
INTELLIGENCE SUMMARY

(Erase heading not required.)

Army Form C. 2118

Place	Date	Hour	Summary of Events and Information	Remarks and references to Appendices
SERDER ROUAG	24/8/1	Weather	Refilling from Supply Column at 10-45 AM Baggage wagons Reformed by firm mile.	(MC
	28/8/1	do	Refilling at 11-30. That 2 of Lt J.D.S Howard A.S.C joined from BHTD T/24784 Pte Howden J Bawdyke HTD to T/102339 Dr H Wills do T/1396 Dr Matthews J from do	(MC
	29/8/1	do	Manual Practice.	(MC
	30/8/1	do	Refilling at 9 AM	(MC
	31/8/1	do	do at 8-30 AM	(MC

Aeroplane Report
Lt H Bryl ? Lt Smith Ham

WAR DIARY
INTELLIGENCE SUMMARY
(Erase heading not required.)

Army Form C. 2118

Place	Date	Hour	Summary of Events and Information	Remarks and references to Appendices
ST MARTIN AU-LAERT	1/7		Weather Showery. Nominal Roll cm ad on H.O. no 80 in charge of this Coy and may Coy nos for W.Dy. Personnel 15 512nd M.V.S. T4/0.59050 Dr Shields I.V admitted 138 et FA T/16 Rennell H.O. 07 79J 270 et Perm't Employment Coy adm N.Y.D.B 138 et FA.	CMC
	2/7		do Nov settles Returned Ringles	CMC
	3/7		do Fire Nymed Rombin, o the ter returning T4/162370 Dy Jordan N returned to duty from L.E. I am informed the	CMC CMC
	4/7		do do	CMC
	5/7		do Mormy R.G.	CMC
	6/7		do Dull T4/SR/01405 L Dr M Wyse On I transferred to the 3rd Coy T4/251986 Cpl.Bn driving A transferred from no 3 Coy	CMC
	7/7		do Fine T4/054450 Dr Shep LV marched to CCS in 31.8°7 201903 Ptohound J 238 Perm' Employment Coy evacuated N.E.S to S.L.1.7	CMC

1875 Wt. W593/826 1,000,000 4/15 J.B.C. & A. A.D.S.S./Forms/C.2118.

WAR DIARY
or
INTELLIGENCE SUMMARY

(Erase heading not required.)

Army Form C. 2118

Place	Date	Hour	Summary of Events and Information	Remarks and references to Appendices
ST MARTIN AU LAERT	8/7/17		Weather Fine. Manuel Rawlins Tr/1×873 Lt Stoll E.A. transferred from Base Depôt (H T & S). Tr/11293 Lt Stoll E.A. transferred to 140 A.T.A.	C.M.C.
	9/7/17		do Fine	C.M.C.
	10/7/17		do Fine. 6 H.D. down from 23rd Mounted Veterinary Hospital, 4 for stray, 1 at 2 for sore leg.	C.M.C.
	11/9/17		do Fine. Lt Small A.S.C. transferred to HQ 41st Train.	C.M.C.
	12/9/17		do Fine	C.M.C.
	13/9/17		do Fair	Baggage wagon dispatched to Brigade now in forward area. Mules led old try in full marching order and found no difficulty at all in walking in a good round trot. Tr/10/91/450 St Shepherd returned to duty.	C.M.C.
ST MARIE CAPPEL	14/9/17		do Fine	HQ & Hq & Supply Section moved to Shelving P.22 A.0.6.	C.M.C.
THIEUSHOUK	15/9/17		do Fine	HQ & Hq & Lorry Section moved to Shelving P.27 S.E. Q.27. D.8.7.	C.M.C.

WAR DIARY or INTELLIGENCE SUMMARY

Army Form C. 2118

Place	Date	Hour	Summary of Events and Information	Remarks and references to Appendices
MILLE KRUISSE	16/7	—	Weather Fine. HQ of Sup. & Supply Section moved to Sheet 17 SW N1A76. Refilling took place at THIEUSHOUK at 9-30AM and after delivery supplies refilling again took place at M1C & KRUISSE at 5pm S/J/34383 Pagate Conaghan from depot H.T.D O/J/102249 St Louders invalided to Base Details sent date 10/7.	(MC
	17/7		do Fair. Refilling in Nye camp at 2-15pm. Filling at OBEROOM outing at noon.	CMC
	18/7		do Dull. Baggage wagon regiment by Lt Brummel Withy. Filling at Gudebrem at 9-20AM. Refilling Nye camp at 10-15AM. Two days outfit delivered to units under extreme materia. T2 and Lt S Corben returned to duty from Base depot H.T.D.	CMC
	19/7		do Fine	CMC
	20/7		do Fine S/J/061028 Pte Penn with AC transferred to Base Depot H.T.D.	CMC
	21/7		do Fine Thomas Ross Inst. Baggage wagon joined unit for transvaal service.	CMC

WAR DIARY
or
INTELLIGENCE SUMMARY
(Erase heading not required.)

Army Form C. 2118

Place	Date	Hour	Summary of Events and Information	Remarks and references to Appendices
BORRE	22/7		HHers & Coy moved to Borre. Multyse W.S.C. 29. Coy moved at 10-0.30 a.m. arrived here at 2 p.m., of Co. settled they inlet 6 p.m.	A/C
	23/7	do	Turtle of Cahn transferred to 19th Bn & Lew Hay at CAESTRE at 9-30 A.M., refilling.	A/C A/C
	24/7	do	Coy camp at 1 hr g Cahn.	A/C
	25/7	do	Return home tu. Coy & waggons reproved units	A/C
	26/7	do	Usual routine.	A/C
			Baggage waggons joined units for Brigade move & Supplies with delivered by S.i.S. Supply Column, refilling in camp at 11 a.m.	A/C
WORMHOUDT	27/7	do	Hers & Coy & Coy moved at 1-30 p.m., of Coy refilling from Supply Column, to WORMHOUDT, arriving at 4-3 pm.	A/C
GHYVELDE	28/7	do	Coy moved to GHYVELDE (Sheet 19 O.1.5.2.8.2.) arriving at 2 p.m., Supplies were delivered to units and refilling from S.i.S Supply by Column took place at 8 p.m.	A/C
	29/7	do	Usual routine, refilling at GHYVELDE at 2 p.m. Coy supply by Column.	A/C
	30/7	do	Filling at ADINKERKE took had at 9 am refilling in camp at 11-30 p.m. (Waggons left O.C. 4 Coy 4, at 5-45 p.m)	A/C

WAR DIARY
or
INTELLIGENCE SUMMARY

(Erase heading not required.)

Army Form C. 2118

Place	Date	Hour	Summary of Events and Information	Remarks and references to Appendices
GHUYELDE	1/9	Weather Fine	Normal Routine. Firing at ADDINKERKE rail head at 9am, 1st sling in Boy's swamp at 1pm. 74/044378/Lieut EVans arm stud military Hospital Parkhurst Nr. London Isle of Wight duty dated 27/9 to return to own men the leave to U.K. and discharged 27/9. Referred who sent 24/9.	(Mc
	2/10/17	do Fine	Normal Routine.	(Mc
	3/10/17	do Fine	7/35647 Pte Bread A transferred from Hdqs to the Coy.	(Mc
	4/10/17	do Rain	74/094209 Pte Henry Coy to Hdqs 1st Siege. Normal Routine. Brisk normal firm orchard. Visited by three. 201373 Pte Russell H, 236 P.E.C. return pte Stopts Cranleigh for tempory re att. 158602 Pte Corporan Jno Gratton 158606 Pte Toplin attached for 126175 Pte Stepping R service in the 305357 Pte Jump JE.	(Mc
	5/10/17	do Fine early later charged to Rain	Normal Routine for 1,2,3 Spade Row. Bagage wagon detached.	(Mc
ST IDES BALDE	6/10/17	do Rain	Hdqs of my moved to ST IDES BALDE. Shut - 11 W18 a 5.5. The Coy moved at 8-30 AM and arrived at midday of the w Shut. Buffetries were delivered to regit.	(Mc
	7/10/17	do Stormy	Summer time ceased at 1am at which time clocks were put back to midnight.	(Mc

WAR DIARY
or
INTELLIGENCE SUMMARY

Army Form C. 2118

(Erase heading not required.)

Places	Date	Hour	Summary of Events and Information	Remarks and references to Appendices
ST IDES BALDE	7/10/17		Rifling took place at 9 am and suitable for Aeroplanes. 9 am met danger at the Ede Kyn down by the Lys. Light railway.	CMC
	8/10/17	March	Wint Ron bee. Cpt Elms left for antigas course at Swinomil Sea school.	CMC
	9/10/17	do	Wint Ron bee. On HD 2s 34 wrong to MyS under date 5/10 for confirmed view.	CMC
	10/10/17	do	Wint Ron bee.	CMC
	11/10/17	Unsettled	Wint Ron bee.	CMC
	12/10/17	Fair	Wint Ron bee. 74/060725 A/c Anderson H Hmm † Cpl	
		Fair	Wint Ron bee. rg/260123 A/c Storey E from CM	
			70/244375 A/BC Cairns M " RCM	
			54/444573 A/St Barker G.A. " Cpl	
			54/060497 A/S Semple E.H. Sgt	
			with A.S.C. letter No 20573	
			dated 12.10.17	
	13/10/17	Rain	Usual Routine	J.S.S
	14/10/17	Fair	Usual Routine	J.S.S
	15/10/17	Fair	Usual Routine	J.S.S
	16/10/17	Fair	Usual Routine	J.S.S
			Refilling time altered to 7 AM.	J.S.S
			1 M.D. chit on change of No 1.G. Co No 69	

WAR DIARY
or
INTELLIGENCE SUMMARY

Army Form C. 2118

Place	Date	Hour	Summary of Events and Information	Remarks and references to Appendices
ST IDESBALDE	17/10/17		Weather Fine. Usual Routine	J.I.S.
	18/10/17		" Fine. Usual Routine	J.I.S.
	19/10/17		" Unsettled. Usual Routine	J.I.S.
	20/10/17		" Fine. Usual Routine	J.I.S.
	21/10/17		" Fine. Usual Routine. No 72/13374 Dr Davis Reinstated T. No T4/215127 Dr Duckenmator S.S. from Base Depot (HTTS) No 72/13874 Dr Drinkwater. T transferred to 140 F.A. No T4/224375 Pte C.P. Evans transferred to No 2 Cy. 201509 Pte Currie. J. of 238 D.L.Cy. Pte D. Donnell E. 201500 transferred to No 2 Cy.	J.I.S.
	22/10/17		" Fine. Usual Routine.	J.I.S.
	23/10/17		" Wet. do	J.I.S.

WAR DIARY
or
INTELLIGENCE SUMMARY

(Erase heading not required.)

Army Form C. 2118

Place	Date	Hour	Summary of Events and Information	Remarks and references to Appendices
ST IDES BALDE	24/10/17		On H.D. no 70 died. On H.D. renewal from _____ Sh/335750 Pte Stephens reinforced from Base Detail. The S.O.C. Visited the Off's camp & inspected horse lines, billets, cook etc.	Dull
	25/10/17		No mad[?] No was late[?]	Cold & Windy / 9.1.1
	26/10/17		On H.D. no 94 died	Wet / 9.1.1
	27/10/17		On H.D. no 25 died	Wet / (MC / (MC)
			Baggage & Luggage Wagons formed route to [?] _____ Staff Coy moved at 3-30 p.m. to LEFFRINCKHOUKE Shut 19 C 29 C.L.I. and arrived at 8 p.m.	Fair
LEFFRINCKHOUKE	28/10/17		T4/237182 St Hair ethn W.K 100 L.F.A.	(MC)
	29/10/17		Fishing at LEFFRINCKHOUKE holding at 10-15 am Rifle Coy in Lop's camp at night.	
	30/10/17		T5/0253891 Q.m. Serlin lut R.J Johnston 138 & J.A	Stormy

WAR DIARY
or
INTELLIGENCE SUMMARY

(Erase heading not required.)

Army Form C. 2118

Place	Date	Hour	Summary of Events and Information	Remarks and references to Appendices
LE FF KING HOUSE	30/10/17	Weather	H.D. Lane No 30 inoculated to 52nd M.V.S.	(MC
	31/10/17	Fine	20.1.721 Reynolds Sergt at R 239 Pour to duty by do 223.853 Daniels Lieut E took admitted 138 d F.A.	(MC

Macgregor Capt.
O.C. 4 Coy 4, or Sus Train

WAR DIARY
INTELLIGENCE SUMMARY
(Erase heading not required.)

Army Form C. 2118

Instructions regarding War Diaries and Intelligence Summaries are contained in F. S. Regs., Part II. and the Staff Manual respectively. Title Pages will be prepared in manuscript.

Place	Date	Hour	Summary of Events and Information	Remarks and references to Appendices
VILLAFRANCA	1 3/8/18		Weather Fine. By Hedgpeth I learned in Cornet at POJANA had had at 5-37 AM in rear of train. Details sound instruction. Boggs Dagan & staff by Wagon to wounded with all the fulton mends. Bofore having made wagon wounded started. Before having made while wounded with return up to + one looking dry Instrument. In train. The Italian Zone tell - the Elements at 8-50 hrs and the journey was not in France. By instructions. In Train. No violent incident.	(MC
In train	2 3/8		do	(MC
do	3 3/8		Hot.	(MC
do	4 3/8		Showing.	(MC
do	5 3/8		Fine. By Officer Detained at MONDICOURT at 8-30 AM and	(MC
WARLUZEL	6 3/8		Fine. Reported to Artillery at MARLUZEL. Boggs Dagan & Supply Wagon of unit which	(MC
—	7 3/8		do. All showed up. of the stray dk number plates T/4 Lt E. MAIN A.S.C. struck off 28/6/78 T/4/057455 Pte Robinson, L. attached 124th Inf/5 Bde H/and was from internment & returned off duty strength.	(MC
—	8 3/8		do. Fine. Made from from T/2nd Lt T. AYANAG H.J. A.S.C. Of... R.S.C. has doit. Italy	(MC

WAR DIARY
or
INTELLIGENCE SUMMARY
(Erase heading not required.)

Army Form C. 2118

Place	Date	Hour	Summary of Events and Information	Remarks and references to Appendices
WARLUZEL	8/3/18	cont[d]	Capt M.B. POLLARD - URQUAHART Transferred to No 3 Coy	(MC
do	9/3/18		Weather Fine. CAPT E.M. TREUTER. A.S.C. transferred from No 3 Coy. Mythical Railway Supply Column at 9-30 p.m.	(MC
do	10/3/18		do Fine. from Groine Railway Column	(MC
do	11/3/18		do Fine. do	(MC
do	12/3/18		Fine. T/158/02198 Pte Howard H.L. admitted 140th F.A. returned to duty	
do	13/3/18		Fine. do	(MC (MC
do	14/3/18		Dull. No T/3/026997 Pte Watson A admitted 140th F.A.	(MC
do	15/3/18		Fine. No T/3/026997 Pte Watson A returned to duty from 140th F.A.	
do	16/3/18		Fine. No Sea Cpl T/18518 to acting Sgt Vacd GS appointed Bath effect from 5.3.17.	(MC
do	17/3/18		Fine. No 308185 Pte Rob off SR 238 "Employment" reg returned to duty from Hospital	(MC (MC

WAR DIARY
INTELLIGENCE SUMMARY

(Erase heading not required.)

Army Form C. 2118

Instructions regarding War Diaries and Intelligence Summaries are contained in F. S. Regs., Part II and the Staff Manual respectively. Title Pages will be prepared in manuscript.

Place	Date	Hour	Summary of Events and Information	Remarks and references to Appendices
WARLUZEL	18/3/18		Weather fine	
do	19/3/18		Wet. Bath(?) ag as an army landed up for the night(?). Above Routine	nil
LOUVENCOURT	20/3/18		Wet. Reville 10am. Coy moved to billets at LOUVENCOURT. T/4/251286 L/Sgt IRVING.A. appointed acting SSM & from forward to 46 Div Train	nil
LAVIGUEVILLE	21/3/18		Fine. Coy moved to billets at LAVIGUEVILLE, rifle at 4pm	nil
ACHIET-LE-PETIT	22/3/18		Fine. Coy moved to ACHIET-LE-PETIT, no refilling took place	nil
do	23/3/18		Fine. Refilling at 11am. T/4/110734 Pte Burbury transferred to 174 I.B. Hqrs	nil
do	24/3/18		Fine. Refilling took place at 9-30am and at from 3pm. Horse-lines were shelled by enemy about 3pm. no casualties. Coy moved to a field about a kilom. the east of BUCQUOY	nil

WAR DIARY or INTELLIGENCE SUMMARY

(Erase heading not required.)

Army Form C. 2118

Place	Date	Hour	Summary of Events and Information	Remarks and references to Appendices
BIENVILLERS AU-BOIS ST AMAND	25/3/18	11 AM 5 p.m.	Weather Fine. By road to BIENVILLERS-AU-BOIS and after to ST AMAND, no refilling took place	(MC
BAILLEUVAL	26/3/18		Weather Fine. By road to BAILLEUVAL about 10·30 A.M. By-passing to observe journey, not order to Brigade of which ordered, refilling took place at ST AMAND before leaving	(MC
do	27/3/18		" Fine. Refilling took place at 2 p.m.	(MC
SAVI-TS	28/3/18		do Nil. By road to SAVI-TS at 9·45 a.m., refilling took place at noon	(MC
AUTHIES	29/3/18		do Fine. By road to AUTHIES after refilling at SAVI-TS.	(MC
—	30/3/18		do Nil. Refilling took place at 10.a.m	(MC
—	31/3/18		do Dull. Refilling took place at 10·30 A.M	(MC

(M.C.McKay)
O.C. 4 Coy 41st Div? Train

WAR DIARY
or
INTELLIGENCE SUMMARY
(Erase heading not required.)

Army Form C. 2118

Place	Date	Hour	Summary of Events and Information	Remarks and references to Appendices
AUTHIES	1/7/8	Weather Dull	Refilling took place at 9-30 pm & 4 pm Regiment to billets at FAMECHON	(ltc
FAMECHON	2/7/8	Fine	Refill at 5 pm	(ltc
PETIT HOUVIN	3/7/8	Wet	Coy HQrs & Supply Section moved to PETIT HOUVIN. Infantry took place in lorries that night at 1-30 pm. Then on my to the job that units returned by the by back returning to different Coy totals.	(ltc
STEENVOORDE	4/7/8	Wet	Entrained at PETIT HOUVIN at 6 am. (Troops & Supply sections travelled with all the tops [units]) detraining at PESELHOEK at 4 pm, from where it marched to billets at STEENVOORDE.	(ltc
—	5/7/8	Wet	Refilling took place at 1 pm, after Supply Wagon. The Gen rolled offier week.	(ltc
—	6/7/8	Wet Dull	Refilling took place at 9 am	(ltc (ltc
VLAMERTINGHE	7/7/8	Fine	Young Railion Coy moved to VLAMERTINGHE	(ltc
—	8/7/8	Fine	Refilling at 9-30 am after a decent supplies were received & dumped & dumped when	(ltc

WAR DIARY
or
INTELLIGENCE SUMMARY

Army Form C. 2118

Place	Date	Hour	Summary of Events and Information	Remarks and references to Appendices
ESTERHOEK	9/4/15		Wheels still Rifling took place at 10-30am Coy moved its tent at ESTERHOEK	(MC
—	10/4/15		Wheels still Rifling at 10-30am	(MC
—	11/4/15		Do Thomp Routine, Rifling in tent at 3pm	(MC
—	12/4/15		Do Horse Run Coy. T3/025684 St. Kirby J T/057737 St. Kirk SR T/278598 St. Metcalfe N G.H.D. Horses 2. 3 Wagon SS T3/106850 St. Bebout M T/14784 St. Horseley 94 H.D. Horses T 2 Wagon SS	all such place to established struck off the strength
—	13/4/15		Do Horse Run Ex, Gunfiring at 2pm	(MC
—	14/4/15		Do Horse Run Coy T4/044653 A/C SM Mulcahy C.J transferred from new Coy 201685 Ptr Howell I 238th Employment by transferred to new Coy 201680 Cpl Henry J 238th Employment by No 3 Coy	(MC

Army Form C. 2118

WAR DIARY
or
INTELLIGENCE SUMMARY

(Erase heading not required.)

Instructions regarding War Diaries and Intelligence Summaries are contained in F.S. Regs., Part II. and the Staff Manual respectively. Title Pages will be prepared in manuscript.

Place	Date	Hour	Summary of Events and Information	Remarks and references to Appendices
ESTERHOEK	15/4/18		Marches fine. Nowt. Rec. tion.	CWC
	16/4/18		Still Nowt. Rec. tion.	CWC
	17/4/18		Still Filling up arranged to H T from rail head was delivered by M T Coke to the top of northern front. Refilling took place the General on the top ramp. See filed on the lye damage, distille Loaves during 14 H T	CWC
	18/4/18		Wet Going to PROVEN at 10 Thes by M T	CWC
	19/4/18		wet Supplies were drawn by M T and of refilling took place at sheen. Some Rations.	CWC
	20/4/18		Fair Nowt. Rations.	CWC
	21/4/18		Fine Nowt. Rations. My lorry & two Lorries inspected by O.C. Train.	CWC
	22/4/18		Fine General Rec tion	CWC
	23/4/18		Fine Nowt. Rec tion. Now to 52nd M.V.S.	CWC
	24/4/18		Fair Still unloading overheads of coy by Lorries at J.A.M. Marched Rec tion.	CWC

1875 Wt. W 593/826 1,000,000 4/15 J.B.C. & A. A.D.S.S./Forms/C. 2118.

WAR DIARY
or
INTELLIGENCE SUMMARY
(Erase heading not required.)

Army Form C. 2118

Place	Date	Hour	Summary of Events and Information	Remarks and references to Appendices
ESTERHOEK	25/7/18	—	Moved route Twnoze. Gs Bustin, S. Bertin Brigade todgis. T/S/83/yyd, Bt wood O.C. Lionsfurd to 124th Infantry Brigade todgis.	O.C.
PESELHOEK AREA	26/7/18	—	Naval Routine. Baggage wagons sent to Scout's Company move to camp in PESELHOEK Area.	J.C.
PROVEN AREA	27/7/18	—	Supplies delivered by M.T. Refilling took place at 1.30 p.m. Company move to camp in PROVEN Area.	J.C.
"	28/7/18	—	Filling by horse transport from PROVEN Railhead at 10.15 a.m. Refilling at 2.0 p.m. Two Lewis recovered from Hanover's taken on strength.	J.C.
"	29/7/18	—	Line of filling at Railhead changed to 9.15 a.m. owing to hostile shelling (no filling at Railhead took place. Supplies delivered by M.T. at 10.0 p.m. and refilling took place at 11.0 p.m.	1.1.1
"	30/7/18	—	Filling took place from M.T. at 10.30 a.m. Refilling at 2.0 p.m.	1.1.1

J.N. Stewart
Lieut for Capt
O.C. 4 Coy. 41st Batt Train

WAR DIARY
or
INTELLIGENCE SUMMARY
(Erase heading not required.)

Army Form C. 2118

Place	Date	Hour	Summary of Events and Information	Remarks and references to Appendices
PROVEN AREA Camp N	1918	—	Weather — Fine	
	2/8	—	Coy moved to camp at F.24.A.6. shot by buffalos were delivered to camp by R.E. Filling took place at 6.0.p.m. and loaded wagons were parked up during the night.	1.J.A.
	3/8	—	" Fine	Supplies were delivered to Units, and refilling took place at 5.30 p.m.	1.J.A.
	4/8	—	" Fine	Usual routine. One to D. Horse No. 6. Knawalid 15 52nd Coy. L. Doing & admitted to Hospital. Ho. 74/250123	1.J.A.
	5/8	—	" Wet.	Usual routine.	1.J.A.
	6/8	—	" Fair.	Usual routine. Baggage Wagons returned from Units. Ho. 126095 Pte. Boffrey J.W. 238th Employment Coy. admitted to Hospital.	1.J.A.
	7/8	—	" Wet.	Filling took place at 9.30 a.m. by C.E. at ROUSBRUGGE railhead to buffalo wagons. Baggage wagons delivering to Units in the event of possible thick mag/when they are to be returned to Units after delivery. Filling at 9.0 p.m. Ho. 73026059 Pte. Rennie (admitted to Hospital.	1.J.A.
	8/8	—	" Fair.	Usual routine. Ho. 186093 Pte. Bottrill R. 258th Employment Coy returned to duty from 139th Field Ambulance.	1.J.A.
	9/8	—	" Fine	Usual routine. No 74/250123, Corpl Blores J. returned to duty from 139th Field Ambulance. Ho. 730646 Pte Potter A. joined from A.D.L. Base Depot and taken on strength.	1.J.A.

WAR DIARY
or
INTELLIGENCE SUMMARY
(Erase heading not required.)

Army Form C. 2118

Place	Date	Hour	Summary of Events and Information	Remarks and references to Appendices
PROVEN AREA CAMP. N.	10/5/18		Weather fine. Usual Routine. Lce Cpl 282/01633. Dr Dowling W. transferred to No 2 Coy.	9.J.9.
	11/5/18		" fair. Usual Routine.	9.1.1.
	12/5/18		" fair. Usual Routine. Camp and tram lines inspected by Divisional Commander.	9.1.1.
	13/5/18		" wet. Usual Routine. 73/02609. Dr Whyte J. evacuated to C.C.S. and struck off strength.	9.1.1.
	14/5/18		" fair. Usual Routine. Lce Cpl Skoletsch, Dr Loden W.A. joined from A.O.B. Base Depot & taken on strength.	9.1.1.
	15/5/18		" fine. Usual Routine. Lce Cpl 05/611. Dr Oakey C. admitted to 139 F Field Amb.	9.1.1.
	16/5/18		" fine. Usual Routine. No T4/011599. Cpl Jakvother, No 1 Company admitted to 139 F Field Amb. No T1/11049. Cpl (A/S/Sgt) Beadle G. promoted to Q.M.S. from 13.11.14. No T3/026937. L.Cpl (A/Cpl) Bowden J. promoted Cpl/oral from 13.11.14.	9.1.1.
	17/5/18		" fine. Usual Routine. 1 O.R. Horse received from Remounts and taken on strength.	9.1.1.
	18/5/18		" fine. Usual Routine.	9.1.1.
	19/5/18 20/5/18		" fine. Usual Routine. Fine. Usual Routine.	9.1.1. 9.1.1.

Army Form C. 2118

WAR DIARY
or
INTELLIGENCE SUMMARY
(Erase heading not required.)

Instructions regarding War Diaries and Intelligence Summaries are contained in F. S. Regs., Part II. and the Staff Manual respectively. Title Pages will be prepared in manuscript.

Place	Date	Hour	Summary of Events and Information	Remarks and references to Appendices
PROVEN AREA CAMP. N.	21/5/8		March Fine Mont Rain	MC
	22/5/8		do do Fine do	MC
	23/5/8		do do Fine do	MC
	24/5/8		do do Wet do	MC
	25/5/8		do do Fine do	MC
	26/5/8		do do Fine do	MC
	27/5/8		do do Fine do J/Bagnall & Wazen dispatched to Shink T/278153 D. Wright transferred from Base Depot	MC
	28/5/8		do do Wet do	MC
	29/5/8		do do Fine do T/136581 artyffe Iwall FM admitted 139 CFA T4/044590 Sgt Bulmer JW admitted 16th FA. Suffering from wounds.	MC
	30/5/8		do do Fine do T4/3R/02198 Dr Howard HL admitted 139 FA T4/3R/02198 Dr Howard ML returned to duty T4/0445/0 Sgt Bulmer JW died of wounds and Struck off the strength	MC
	31/5/8		do do Fine do	MC

J.M. Colgrove Capt
O.C. 4 Coy 41st Div. Train

WAR DIARY
INTELLIGENCE SUMMARY

Army Form C. 2118

Place	Date	Hour	Summary of Events and Information	Remarks and references to Appendices
CAMP N SLIGY FLYA	1/6/18	Nil	Nominal Roll. T/36581 Rfg Gee Small TM evacuated to C.C.S	CMC
—	2/6/18	do	Nominal Roll. Brigade Wagn despatched to unit T/40516281 Dehny Ry returned 15 July from 138 HTA	CMC
BOLEZEELE 3/6/18	do	do	Ry Headquarters and Supply section moved to billets from BOLEZEELE with Brigade transport.	CMC
BROUERES 4/6/18	do	do	Ry Headquarters and Supply section moved to BROUERES Brigade transport remaining at unit "en route"	CMC
—	5/6/18	do	Nominal Roll.	CMC
—	6/6/18	do	T/6239471 Sgt Scott N.P. joined from Base Depot.	CMC
—	7/6/18	do	Ration from London Gazette Supplement 30/5/18 Intimated on subject Capt. J.H. Colquhoun No 4 Coy Supplies drawn by H.Q. from WATTEN	CMC
—	8/6/18	do	Baggage & wagon formed into Brigade train. Rfg Chaply of the J. Duffy detail arrived at HERICAT	CMC

1875 Wt. W593/826 1,000,000 4/15 J.B.C. & A. A.D.S.S./Forms/C. 2118.

WAR DIARY

INTELLIGENCE SUMMARY

Army Form C. 2118

Place	Date	Hour	Summary of Events and Information	Remarks and references to Appendices
HERICAT	9/6/15		Supplies were drawn by MT T/088605 Dr Guymer JW found from Base Depot to Jehyctock No. 2 F.A. Extract from Engineer Supplement dated 3/6/15 awarded Distinguished Conduct Service Medal, No T4/213880 SSM Foxley L.A. No 4 Cy Hd Divisional Train	(MC
BONNINGUES	10/6/15		Coy Head Quarters & Supply Section moved to BONNINGUES. Baggage wagon reported from units	(MC
—	11/6/15		Moved Rations	(MC
—	12/6/15		T/31/3063 Pte Talbot A admitted No 9 FA	(MC
—	13/6/15		Usual Routine	(MC
			Usual Routine No 20184/6 Pte Ingraham E returned to C/238 Employment Coy No 201707 Pte Lusch " " No 405611 Pte Hopkins S } found from No 36553 Pte Hotchen W } 238 Employment Coy	(MC
—	14/6/15		Fine Usual Routine	(MC

Army Form C. 2118

WAR DIARY
or
INTELLIGENCE SUMMARY
(Erase heading not required.)

Instructions regarding War Diaries and Intelligence Summaries are contained in F. S. Regs., Part II. and the Staff Manual respectively. Title Pages will be prepared in manuscript.

Place	Date	Hour	Summary of Events and Information	Remarks and references to Appendices
BONNINGUES	15/6/18	—	Weather Fine. Normal Routine. 7/313063 Pte Talbot A returned to duty from 140 th F.A.	(H.C.
—	16/6/18		— Normal Routine.	(H.C.
—	17/6/18		Fine Normal Routine.	(H.C.
—	18/6/18		Fine Normal Routine. 36553 Pte Hobden W 238 th Employment Coy admitted 140 th Field Ambulance.	(H.C.
—	19/6/18		Fine Normal Routine.	(H.C.
—	20/6/18		Fine Normal Routine. 36553 Pte Hobden W 238 th Employment Coy evacuated to No. 11 C.C.S.	(H.C.
—	21/6/18		Fine Normal Routine. T1/1/12 St Butler JH admitted 140 th F.A. suffering from	(H.C.
—	22/6/18		Fine Normal Routine. S4/090398 Pte Butler CH M admitted 140 th T4/233821 Dr Pery AF T3/4619 M L Dr Raleigh J } F.A. suffering from influenza. The following evacuated to No. 11 C.C.S. suffering from influenza.	(H.C.

1875 Wt. W593/825 1,000,000 4/15 J.B.C. & A. A.D.S.S./Forms/C. 2118.

WAR DIARY
INTELLIGENCE SUMMARY
(Erase heading not required.)

Army Form C. 2118.

Place	Date	Hour	Summary of Events and Information	Remarks and references to Appendices
BOURINGUES	23/6/18		Weather Fine. Normal Routine. To/344498 A/Cpl Clerenbell G/went from	
			Base Depot to J.S.C.	
			Bom Depot ASC	
			S/314096 Pte Wro JH) admitted to	
			To/02702 Dr McEvoy T) No of JA	(MC
			Tu/10609 24 Cpl Sackey JH	
			Tu/059720 Pte Stanley J returned to duty	
	24/6/18		Weather Fine. Normal Routine. Baggage Wagon formed up for Brigade	
			movie.	
			S/4/070291 Pte Collipp NS) admitted	
			T3/023137 Dr Hugh L J)	
			TS/9608 MI to Cracken JA) No of JA	(MC
			S/143837 Pte Crockey J)	
			S/307256 Pte Budd F)	
			T4/094233 Dr Heritage BH	
BROEKE	25/6/18		Weather Fine. Normal Routine. Coy Hdqrs & Supply Sub Sections moved to	
			KEUSE to BROERE	(MC

WAR DIARY or INTELLIGENCE SUMMARY

Army Form C. 2118.

Place	Date	Hour	Summary of Events and Information	Remarks and references to Appendices
BROERE	25/6/18		Capt E.M. Truter, RAMC admitted 140th FA	AE
			T/7987 Dmr .... do	
			T/194765 Pte Wyburgh do	
OUDEZEELE	26/6/18		Much from Abeel Rusken Coy HQrs & Supply section moved to OUDEZEELE from refugee huts. Horse lines moved to Sn. L of J. Clemens	
			T3/023359 to Hosp J.	
			T4/SR/021985 H...... S....	admitted
			S4/060014 Sgt Inglis C.C.S	
			T5/9149 Walbach Patrick CE 140 FA	
			T5/7685 Whelehan Chr J	
			T/367192 Leir Kirby	
			T/361151 Cornwell H	
			T/32953	
			207/y4 235 Pte Hanford	
			T5/026930 L/Cpl Freeman Wortimal to duty from 36 CCS	AE

Army Form C. 2118.

WAR DIARY
or
INTELLIGENCE SUMMARY.
(Erase heading not required.)

Place	Date	Hour	Summary of Events and Information	Remarks and references to Appendices
OUDEZEELE	27/6		Muster Time Marol Roubins T4/052590 L/Cpl Barry J W T4/022927 Pte Liddell J W T/261025 Farrier St Sadler M J T5/8697 Saddler St/Cpl S/S A Holmes	admitted 140 & FA (Me)
	28/6		Muster Time Marol Roubins T4/143056 Saddler St/Cpl H W T/35638 Dr Ivy W M S T4/065213 Dr Harvey C R	admitted 140 & FA (Me)
	29/6		Neither Time Marol Roubins Suffice was down by H.T. from STEENVOORDE at noon, nothing took place in camp at 2-30 pm.	(Me)
	30/6		Muster Time Marol Roubins	

(signature)
O.C. 4 Coy Hnd Div Train

WAR DIARY
INTELLIGENCE SUMMARY.
(Erase heading not required.)

Army Form C. 2118.

Place	Date	Hour	Summary of Events and Information	Remarks and references to Appendices
STEENVOORDE	1/5		Weather fine. Moved Rwn. Coy. H.Q. round to billets at STEENVOORDE	
			T/1/712 Pte Butler J.H.	
			TS/4619 W/s Raleigh S } Returned to duty from Hospital	(HC
			T4/235621 Dvr. Parr A.R.	
			Moved Rwn. Baggage wagon refused from escort	
	2/5		do refusing had placed under escort at 2 p.m.	
			T4/105290 Dvr. Bergin J	
			T/132953 Dvr. ..... L.E.	
			T4/143066 Saddler Sgt. ..... H.W. } Returned to duty from Hospital	(HC
			T/35633 Dvr. Hoyles W/S	
			T4/062213 Dvr. M..... C.R.	
			T/261085 Farrier St..... H.G.	
	3/5		do Moved Rwn. Coy.	
			A/533 Dvr. Wilkes L.J.	
			T/260768 St. Harte..... J } Joined from Base Depot H.T.S.S.	(HC
			T/418511 Dvr. Jervis S.	

WAR DIARY
INTELLIGENCE SUMMARY
(Erase heading not required.)

Army Form C. 2118.

Place	Date	Hour	Summary of Events and Information	Remarks and references to Appendices
STEENVOORDE	3/7/18 Cont'd		T/36768 St Hutchison J } Transferred to	(HE
			T/418511 St Jarvis S } 140 of J.A.	
	4/7/18		Marches Stun Manual Routes	
			S/060014 Sgt Jackson C.L.	
			Tu/60725 L/Cpl Lindow JH	
			S4/070398 Pte Burton CHM	
			S4/070291 Pte Cartledge HS	Returned to duty
			T/36857 St Colwil JH	
			S/314096 Pte Evans JH	from Hospitals
			T3/023139 St Heath CJ	(HE
			TS/027005 St McGregor J	
			TS/7608 Wheeler St Goodlet JA.	
			201904 Pte Steinfield J	
			(236 Employment Coy)	

WAR DIARY
INTELLIGENCE SUMMARY

Army Form C. 2118.

Place	Date	Hour	Summary of Events and Information	Remarks and references to Appendices
STEENVORDE	5/7/18		Weather fine.	
			T3/028859 Dr Hogg }	
			T4/158/02198 Dr Hockley H.E. } Evacuated to 64th C.C.S. on 2/6/18	
			T1/3984 Dr Murray J.	
			S/343837 Pte Carrothers (M.H.) Evacuated to 36th C.C.S on 24/6/18	
			T4/094235 Dr Hurley (M.H.)	
			S/307256 Pte Small J.	
			T/36792 L/Cpl Kerr L.J.	
			T5/9149 Saddler Cpl Fetwick C.E. } Evacuated to 2nd Canadian C.C.S. on 26/6/18	
			T5/9685 Wheeler Cpl Simmonds A.	M.C.
—	6/7/18		Weather fine. Major Dunn to billets was inspected by G.O.C. Division at 9-30 A.M.	
			S/302605 Pte Whyte C.J. returned to duty from C.C.S. and called on the strength of	M.C.
—	7/7/18		Weather fine. Normal Routine.	M.C.
—	8/7/18		Weather fine. Normal Routine. T5/9225 Saddler Cpl marked P form no 1 Cog. T3/08906 S/Sergt Maguire J admitted to 138 at F.A.	M.C.

WAR DIARY
INTELLIGENCE SUMMARY.
(Erase heading not required.)

Army Form C. 2118.

Place	Date	Hour	Summary of Events and Information	Remarks and references to Appendices
STEENVOORDE	9/7/18	—	Weather fine. Naval Review	(HC
—	10/7/18	—	Weather wet. do	(HC
—	11/7/18	—	Weather wet. A Full marching order parade of other ranks Inspected at 2-30pm by O.C. Coy, who in the event Re-inspected by him S/343837 Pte Carmichael J T/5/094235 St Heritage J/H T/0/23359 St H.T.W.A. T/5/8/04198 St H.T.M.W. Sgt Dt T/5/8697 St Murray J S/307256 Pte Meadle H.	(HC
—	12/7/18	—	Weather wet. Naval Review T/5/8697 Sadler left Witnol S.J.C. 2nd Friendly 23/9/18	(HC
—	13/7/18	—	do Fine Naval Review Capt F.H.TRUTER A.S.C. invalided to U.K. 30/6/18	(HC
—	14/7/18	—	do Fine Naval Review T3/024005 Dr Bingley J returned to duty from 138 A.F.A.	(HC
—	15/7/18	—	do Fine Naval Review	(HC

WAR DIARY
INTELLIGENCE SUMMARY.
(Erase heading not required.)

Army Form C. 2118.

Instructions regarding War Diaries and Intelligence Summaries are contained in F. S. Regs., Part II. and the Staff Manual respectively. Title pages will be prepared in manuscript.

Place	Date	Hour	Summary of Events and Information	Remarks and references to Appendices
STEENVOORDE	16/7/18		Windy Fair. Manual Routine	CWC
	17/7/18		Fair. T/278153 St. Wright W admitted 138 ⅋ FA.	CWC
			do. Returned to duty	CWC
	18/7/18		Fine. Baggage wagon left Coy to join convoy. Manual Routine	CWC
	19/7/18		Fine. Capt. E.S. Meacham A.S.C. joined from 37 Railhead Supply Det. Manual Routine	CWC
	20/7/18		Fine. T/3/869 Saddler Staff Sgt. E. Arthur D. returned to duty from H.Q. Staff. T/3/4.685 Sgt. Seaman to H.J. Attached from S.C. Sec Lnl Kirby & taken on Strength of Coy col	CWC
	21/7/18		Fair. Manual Routine	CWC
	22/7/18		Fine. Manual Routine T/278153 Dr. Wright W admitted to 138 ⅋ FA.	CWC
	23/7/18		Fine. Manual Routine T/3/6792 L/cpl Kirby J. trans to 75 Permanent Base details on admission to Hospital 26/6/18.	CWC
			Gde. T/cloud. on admission to local base details. T/3/6792 L/Cpl Kirby J. off roll of Coy contd.	CWC
	24/7/18		Fine. Manual Routine T/278153 Dr Wright W joined from 58th CCS	CWC

WAR DIARY

INTELLIGENCE SUMMARY.

Army Form C. 2118.

Place	Date	Hour	Summary of Events and Information	Remarks and references to Appendices
STEENVORDE	25/7	Weekly Tour	Mounted Route 7/5/69 to Rebuy Mount Route from A.S.C Branch Depot to 140th S.A.	(M.C
—	26/7	do	Mount Route 2 Supply Wagon reported for 1st Bn 106th American Inf Reg & and 105 th (M Rly) Ammo Train 7/5/69 the J.J.	(M.C
			Two new Sam Battalions attachment	
			Reports 16/3 Pte from Sgt Gardner from A.S.C	(M.C
—	27/7	do	Mount Route	(M.C
—	28/7	do	Mount Route	(M.C
—	29/7	do	Mount Route	(M.C
—	30/7	do	Mount Route Iss Supply Wagon to 4th Canadian	(M.C
—	31/7	do	Transport Rifles issued for attachment	(M.C
			Mount Route	(M.C

(M.C) Capt
O.C. 4 Coy 41st Div Train

WAR DIARY
or
INTELLIGENCE SUMMARY.

(Erase heading not required.)

Army Form C. 2118.

Place	Date	Hour	Summary of Events and Information	Remarks and references to Appendices
STEENVOORDE	1/6/18	—	Weather Fine. Noval Review. Baggage wagons returned from moves	
			2 Supply wagons of 106 (Yorks) amoured M.G. Batty	
			returned for attachment	
	2/6/18		2 Supply wagons 103rd (Yorks) amoured M.G. Batty	(AE
			returned for attachment	
			Weather Wet. Noval Review. No T/178153 Pte Boylett W.	(AE
	3/6/18		returned to R.S.C. Base Depot for the discharges.	
			Weather Wet. Noval Review Board	(AE
			by Standing Medical Board	
			2 Noval Motor Tow Supply Wagons of 106 Armoured	
			Infantry Regt (1st Batty) returned Glenmarit	
			on supply wagon of 1st Batty 108 & 2nd Regt	(AE
	4/8/18		Joined for attachment	
			Weather Fair. Noval Review. No T/304631 Pte Hayes A.F.	
	5/8/18		proceeded to R.S.C. Base Depot (surplus to establishment)	(AE
	6/8/18		Weather Wet. Noval Review.	
			Weather Wet. Noval Review. No T/36792 L/cpl Keith J. appointed	

WAR DIARY
or
INTELLIGENCE SUMMARY.
(Erase heading not required.)

Army Form C. 2118.

Place	Date	Hour	Summary of Events and Information	Remarks and references to Appendices
STEENVORDE	6/8/15	cont.	acting L/Cpl retd. pay from 20.7.15	(see
	7/8/15		Weather Fair. Usual Routine	(see
	8/8/15		do. do.	(see
	9/8/15		do. Usual Routine	(see
	10/8/15		do. Usual Routine T4/313446 Dr Oustham HW joined from T4/23609 Dr Purrough H }Base Depot T/39023u Dr Parket H T5/9149 Saddler Cpl Petrick CE HT&S	(see
			On Supply Wagon of 1st Battn 108th Inf Regt returned to unit	
	11/8/15	do.	Weather Fine T4/086395 Dr Tavener A joined from Base Depot A.S.C. (HT&S). Two Supply Wagons of 1st Battn 108 American Inf. Regt joined for attachment	(see
	12/8/15	do.	Usual Routine T1/112 Dr Battiwell H } Joined from T/36851 Dr Leffcoat H A.S.C. (Base Depot T/2726 Dr Griffin J (HT&S) T/32935 Dr Morris E T/36236 Dr Murray WH	(see

WAR DIARY or INTELLIGENCE SUMMARY

Army Form C. 2118.

Place	Date	Hour	Summary of Events and Information	Remarks and references to Appendices
STEENVOORDE	13/8	March Past	Mount Rouler	(MC
—	14/8	do Fine	do	(MC
—	15/8	do Fine	T/370.493 St Perry Duf from A S C Base Depot	(MC
—	16/8	do Fine	do	(MC
—	17/8	do Fair	do	(MC
—	18/8	do Fine	do	(MC
—	19/8	do Fine	Duffy Major & 3rd Batt 108th Infty Hanover & Duffy Major & 104th Inb American U.S. Cay reported school units	(MC
—	20/8	do Fine	do	(MC
—	21/8	do Fine	do	1.1
—	22/8	do Fine	do	1.1
—	23/8	do Fine	do	1.1
—	24/8	do Dull	do	1.1
—	25/8	do Fine	To/9.333. Lbadd: Coyl baker returned to O.S.S. Base Depot, surplus to establishment. Cant. Jones instructed by O.C. train.	1.1

WAR DIARY
or
INTELLIGENCE SUMMARY.
(Erase heading not required.)

Army Form C. 2118.

Place	Date	Hour	Summary of Events and Information	Remarks and references to Appendices
STEENVOORDE	26/8	—	Weather Wet. Usual Routine.	1/1/1
"	27/8	—	" 2 Buffalo & 2 Baggage Wagons of W° Qd.t Div. L. Batt. joined 123rd M.T. Coy.	1/1/1
"	28/8	—	" Wet.	
"	"	—	Usual Routine. Buffalo wagon of 234 Field Coy R.E. joined 123rd M.T. Coy.	1/1/1
"	"	—	Buffalo wagon of 228 Field Ambulance R.E. joined.	1/1/1
"	29/8	—	Usual Routine. Buffalo wagon of M° Field Ambulance joined.	1/1/1
"	"	—	Unit.	1/1/1
"	30/8	—	Usual Routine. Baggage wagon & Supply Unit for Brigade leaves.	1/1/1
PERENNE	31/8	—	" " Hdqtrs and Supply Section travel to Petorie at PERENNE	1/1/1
			Usual Routine.	

T. A. Nimrod Lieut & Capt.
O.C. H.Q. 41st Divl. train A.S.C.

WAR DIARY
or
INTELLIGENCE SUMMARY
(Erase heading not required.)

Army Form C. 2118.

Instructions regarding War Diaries and Intelligence Summaries are contained in F. S. Regs., Part II. and the Staff Manual respectively. Title pages will be prepared in manuscript.

Place	Date	Hour	Summary of Events and Information	Remarks and references to Appendices
STEENVOORDE	1/8	Weather Fine	Manual Rations. Supplies were delivered to Camp by M.T.	(inc
—	2/9/18	do	M.T. Manual Rations. Supplies delivered to Camp by M.T.	(atc
—	3/9/18	do	Supply wagon of 2nd M.S. Battn. formed up after lunch. Manual Rations. Supplies delivered by M.T. to Coy. 2/Lt J CAVANAGH admitted 120th F.A. on Aug 27 of 31½ inch	(inc
—	4/9/18	do	Khaki on march kit 3/8. Manual Rations. Baggage wagon reformed by fire arms.	(inc
—	5/9/18	do	Ration drawn from WINNEZEELE at 11 AM by H.T. Refilling in camp.	(inc
—	6/9/18	do	Manual Rations	(inc
WIPPENHOEK	7/9/18	do Wet	Coy moved to Hill site at Shut 27 L 23 A.5.2. Supplies drawn by H.T. from WIPPENHOEK at 8.15 AM Refilling in Camp	(inc
—	8/9/18	do Wet	Manual Rations.	(inc

WAR DIARY
or
INTELLIGENCE SUMMARY

Army Form C. 2118.

Place	Date	Hour	Summary of Events and Information	Remarks and references to Appendices
WIPPENHOEK	9/8		Weather Wet. About Routine	OiC
	10/8		do Wet. About Routine to Tr/a 59 T.C. to Standby & submitted Eighties R.S.	CHC
	11/8		do Wet. Supplies as usual drawn from WIPPENHOEK Rail head at 10.3. A.M. Tr. I + V CATANACH returned to	(HC
	12/8		do Wet. duty from TIS to to that Store	(HC
	13/8		do Wet. Baggage wagon formed route for Brigade move Supply & Baggage wagon of 141 & 173 Btns Joined 2 Coy & Supply Column 228 Artillery Bge CRE formed 3 Coy	CHC
LEDERZEELE 14/8		do Wet. Coy Headquarters & Supply Section moved to LEDERZEELE (STAGING AREA) 1 Rated No 6 reserve Coy to B 52 and M.V.S. took Church	(HC
CLEAQUES 15/8		do Fair. All the strong &c Coy Headquarters & Supply Section moved to CLEAQUES. Refilling took place	CHC

Army Form C. 2118.

WAR DIARY
or
INTELLIGENCE SUMMARY.
(Erase heading not required.)

Instructions regarding War Diaries and Intelligence Summaries are contained in F. S. Regs., Part II. and the Staff Manual respectively. Title pages will be prepared in manuscript.

Place	Date	Hour	Summary of Events and Information	Remarks and references to Appendices
CUERAVES	15/8		Weather fine. At 3pm rod wire and supplies were delivered to units in they arrived. A mech refill of ammunition of 100 Flare, outfits delivered to Coy. by M.T.	
—	16/8		Weather fine. Major Robertson	(MC
—	17/8		Weather fine. do	(MC
—	18/8		Weather fine. do	(MC
—	19/8		Weather fine. do T/306,70 Lt Potter A. admitted to 10 Stationary Hospital	(MC
—	20/8		Weather fine. do The rations were delivered by Supply Column to an bivouac of ration wagon to units. Supply Column lorry moved up rations.	(MC
—	21/8		Weather fine. do T4/044653 S/s a/C.S.M Mulcahy J. promoted C.S.M.	(MC

WAR DIARY
or
INTELLIGENCE SUMMARY.
(Erase heading not required.)

Army Form C. 2118.

Place	Date	Hour	Summary of Events and Information	Remarks and references to Appendices
CLERQUES	22/7/18	Marched Past	Baggage + road ends for Brigade over. 7/11th Batt. S.M. joined from A.S.C. Base Depot.	Cre
	23/7/18	Marched Past	Normal Routine	Cre
	24/7/18	Marched Past	Normal Routine	Cre
	25/7/18	Marched Past	do	Cre
RUBROUCQ	26/7/18	Marched Past	Cy. Hd.qrs. & Supply Section moved to RUBROUCQ	Cre
WIPPENHOEK	27/7/18	Marched Past	Cy. Hd.qrs. & Supply Section moved to WIPPENHOEK – 6.29 C.8.2. Strs. 27. Arrived from 14/2157 St Sachmen to 8/2 & 140 CField Ambulance + returned. Offals along Co.	Cre
BRANDHOEK	28/7/18	Marched Past	Rlk'n. Cap'l. Hd.qrs. & Supply Section moved to believe & SMQ 28 G 11. c. central.	Cre
	29/7/18	Marched Past	Normal Routine. Supply his delivered to Cy. by M.T.	Cre
	30/7/18	Marched Past	Normal Routine	Cre

Macgwire Capt.
O.C. # Coy 4 Jo. Div. Train

Army Form C. 2118.

WAR DIARY
or
INTELLIGENCE SUMMARY.
(Erase heading not required.)

Place	Date	Hour	Summary of Events and Information	Remarks and references to Appendices
VOORMEZEELE	1/10/18	Marches etc	Coy Headquarters & Supply Section moved to VOORMEZEELE	C in C
—	2/10/18	Marches etc	Moved Rations Refilling Pt to place at Coy Camp	C in C
—	3/10/18	Marches etc	" Capt E.S. MEEHAN ASC admitted 36 Stationary Hospital sick	C in C
—	4/10/18	Marches etc	"	C in C
—	5/10/18	Marches etc	" 7/30 b/c to Pkt A reverted to N.Z. Infantry. Hostile G attack off the to hong it	C in C
—	6/10/18	Marches etc	" Supply wagon of 136 N.Z.F.A. 4 & 27 Field Coy R.E. joined for attachment	C in C
POPERINGHE	7/10/18	Marches etc	" Coy Hqrs & Supply Section moved to billets at Pope'inghe	C in C
—	8/10/18	Marches etc	" On Railhead Current from Soman to y Charma eh at Army Ch	C in C
—	9/10/18	Marches etc	"	C in C
—	10/10/18	Marches etc	"	C in C
HULHOEK	11/10/18	Marches etc	" Coy & Section moved to Shit 27 B 2+0 S.7	C in C

WAR DIARY
or
INTELLIGENCE SUMMARY.
(Erase heading not required.)

Army Form C. 2118.

Place	Date	Hour	Summary of Events and Information	Remarks and references to Appendices
HILLHOEK	12/9/17		Weather fair. Left the men lines by H.T. from VLAMERTINGE - without Baggage. Baggage found cart of the Bgd. arr.	(R/c
YPRES	13/9/17		Weather wet. Gty & left by T.L. for a night to billets at Shut 2d I.M.C.S.A. Staff be will repair from VLAMERTINGHE by H.T.	(R/c
—	14/9/17		Weather fine. Moved Rations. Supplies drawn by M.T. from TROIS ROIS. Billets adjoining at T.I.S.A.	(R/c
—	15/9/17		Weather fair. Usual routine. No Tabasso. Sgt. Booker W. to joined from A.O.C. Base Depot.	1/2
DADIZEELE	16/9/17		" Usual routine. Two Sadoys T Buffalo Section moved to Billets at DADIZEELE.	1/2
—	17/9/17		" Buffalos drawn by M.T. from TROIS ROIS & returned to Units.	1/2
—	18/9/17		" Usual routine. 1 G.D. he had admitted to 32nd F.A.S. Personal lot a Supplies delivered by M.T. and wounded.	1/2
—	19/9/17		" Usual routine.	1/2

Army Form C. 2118.

WAR DIARY
or
INTELLIGENCE SUMMARY.
(Erase heading not required.)

Instructions regarding War Diaries and Intelligence Summaries are contained in F. S. Regs., Part II. and the Staff Manual respectively. Title pages will be prepared in manuscript.

Place	Date	Hour	Summary of Events and Information	Remarks and references to Appendices
MOORSEELE	20/9/18	—	Weather wet. Usual routine. Coys todays & Butt'n Section move to Billets at MOORSEELE.	1 L
BISINGHEM	21/9/18	—	" fair. Usual routine. Coys todays & Butt'n Section move to Billets at BISINGHEM.	1 L
"	22/9/18	—	" " Usual routine.	1 L
"	23/9/18	—	" " Usual routine.	1 L
"	24/9/18	—	" " Usual routine. No. 236099 Pte Carson (to. evacuated to 6.6.5. 25/9 - Gun of strength.	1 L
"	25/9/18	—	" " Usual routine.	1 L
"	26/9/18	—	" " Usual routine.	1 L
"	27/9/18	—	" " Usual routine. Splitting took place at 7.30 a.m. Supplies were delivered to Units. A second lot as Supplies were drawn to the S.J. from LEDEGHEM Railhead. Baggage wagons gone Unit.	1 L
"	28/9/18	—	" " Usual routine.	1 L
COURTRAI	29/9/18	—	" " Company moved to Billets at COURTRAI. Supplies were drawn by R.J. from BISSEGHEM Railhead.	1 L

WAR DIARY
or
INTELLIGENCE SUMMARY

(Erase heading not required.)

Army Form C. 2118.

Place	Date	Hour	Summary of Events and Information	Remarks and references to Appendices
COURTRAI	30.11.18	—	Weather fine. Usual routine. 2nd Lieuts. MITCHELL W.G. and Lt. 632803 - Lt. WORSICK T.W. joined from 230? Employment Coy.	1, 2
	31.12.18	—	Usual routine	
			Kavanagh Lieut. for Col. O.C. 11th Bn. Joint Irish Div. Q.O.B.	

Army Form C. 2118.

WAR DIARY
or
INTELLIGENCE SUMMARY.
(Erase heading not required.)

Instructions regarding War Diaries and Intelligence Summaries are contained in F. S. Regs., Part II. and the Staff Manual respectively. Title pages will be prepared in manuscript.

Place	Date	Hour	Summary of Events and Information	Remarks and references to Appendices
COURTRAI	1/1/18	Whole day Fine	Manual Routine. Ration drawn by M.T from BISSEGHEM	I.C
SYEVEGHEM	2/1/18	do Fine	Shifted	
			Coy HQs & Supply Sections moved to billets near SYEVEGHEM. Manual Routine.	I.C
	3/1/18	do Fine	Manual Routine.	I.C
	4/1/18	do Fine	do	I.C
DEERLYCK	5/1/18	do Wet	Coy HQs moved to billets at I.33.A.9.6. Sheet 29. Manual Routine	(MC
	6/1/18	do Fine	do	(MC
	7/1/18	do Wet	Coy HQs moved to billets at Sheet 29. I.9.B.4.5.	(MC
	8/1/18	do Wet	Manual Routine. Supplies were delivered by M.T	(MC
	9/1/18	do Fine	Rations drawn by M.T from Vic. H.T.E Shed head	(HC
INGOYGHEM	10/1/18	do Fine	Manual Routine. Coy HQs moved to billets at INGOYGHEM. Rations was delivered by M.T.	(WC
BERKHEM	11/1/18	do Wet	Coy Head quarters moved to billets at BERKHEM where were delivered by wagon of H1.O. DAC Manual Routine.	(MC
	12/1/18	do Fine	Manual Routine.	

Army Form C. 2118.

WAR DIARY
or
INTELLIGENCE SUMMARY.
(Erase heading not required.)

Instructions regarding War Diaries and Intelligence Summaries are contained in F. S. Regs., Part II. and the Staff Manual respectively. Title pages will be prepared in manuscript.

Place	Date	Hour	Summary of Events and Information	Remarks and references to Appendices
BERKHEM	12/7/18	Con.td	T4/060725 Cpl Sanders JH appointed a/Sgt	
	13/7/18	—	T4/058590 Pte Bury JJR appointed a/L/Cpl. Weather fair. Usual Routine	C in C
	14/7/18	—	No. 2 Coy moved to billets at NEDERBRAKEL, relieved by M.T.	C in C
NEDERBRAKEL	14/7/18		Relieved by M.T.	
	15/7/18	—	Usual Routine	C in C
	16/7/18	—	T4/234472 Sgt Scott WP transferred to No 1 Coy. T4/36742 a/L/Cpl Kirk J there of Coy. T4/211173 L/Cpl Coe G army 2nd Coy. Usual Routine	C in C
	16/7/18	—	T4/1392 L.Cpl Matthews J died in 53rd General Hospital of wounds received 8.7.18 whilst on the Convoy to Supply Mayors of 1.89 Fd Bgde R.F.A. Usual Routine	C in C
	17/7/18	—	Usual Routine	C in C
MEERSCHVOORDE	18/7/18	—	No 2 Coy moved to billets at MEERSCHVOORDE	C in C / T in C

Army Form C. 2118.

WAR DIARY
or
INTELLIGENCE SUMMARY.
(Erase heading not required.)

Instructions regarding War Diaries and Intelligence Summaries are contained in F. S. Regs., Part II. and the Staff Manual respectively. Title pages will be prepared in manuscript.

Place	Date	Hour	Summary of Events and Information	Remarks and references to Appendices
MEERSCHHOEKDE	19/11	Needles	Firm and Rubin	C/we
VIANE	20/11	do	Coy moved to billets at VIANE	C/we
—	21/11	do	do and Rine line	C/we
—	22/11	do	do	C/we
—	23/11	do	do	C/we
—	24/11	do	do	C/we
—	25/11	do	do	C/we
—	26/11	do	do	C/we
—	27/11	Still	do	C/we
—	28/11	Not	T/1878 L/Cpl a/L/Sgt Norton J.S. promoted Temp/Sgt. with effect from 3/11	C/we
—	29/11	Firm	do	C/we
—	30/11	Wet	do	C/we

Intelligence Officer
O.C. 4 Coy 41st Bn. E. Surrey

WAR DIARY
or
INTELLIGENCE SUMMARY.

(Erase heading not required.)

Army Form C. 2118.

Place	Date	Hour	Summary of Events and Information	Remarks and references to Appendices
VIANE	1/10	—	Muster Roll. Moved Rendez-vous Billeting at 8-45 a.m in VIANE.	C/HC
—	2/10	—	do. do.	C/HC
—	3/10	—	do. do.	C/HC
—	4/10	—	do. do.	C/HC
—	5/10	—	do. do.	C/HC
—	6/10	—	do. do.	C/HC
—	7/10	—	do. do.	C/HC
—	8/10	—	do. do.	C/HC
—	9/10	—	do. do.	C/HC
—	10/10	—	do. 405611 Pte Hutchen G. 238 Empl Coy att from Labour Corps.	C/HC
—	11/10	—	do. Brig. Orders. Lt/Maj Wynne 107 Bde RFA confirmed as 2/i/c	C/HC
—	12/10	—	do. Lt Col Hope & Supply Officers moved to billets at ENGHIEN	C/HC
ENGHIEN	12/10	—		C/HC

WAR DIARY
or
INTELLIGENCE SUMMARY

(Erase heading not required.)

Army Form C. 2118.

Place	Date	Hour	Summary of Events and Information	Remarks and references to Appendices
HAM	13/12/18	—	Weather dull. Coy HQrs & Supply Section moved to billets at HAM. S/24321 Pte Crombrey admitted 140 it F.A.	(MC)
WATERLOO	14/12/18	—	Weather fair. Coy HQrs & Supply Section moved to WATERLOO. 25/26737 Cpl Knowlen F. evacuated to 55th C.C.S.	(MC)
	15/12/18	—	do. Normal Routine	(MC)
GENAPPE	16/12/18	—	do. Coy HQrs & Supply Section moved to Bablette nr GENAPPE. T3/027001 Sgt Scully J. admitted 140 F.A.	(MC)
BRYE	17/12/18	—	do. Coy HQrs & Supply Section moved to BRYE. T3/027001 Sgt Scully J. evacuated to 53rd CCS	(MC)
TEMPLOUX	18/12/18	—	Wet. Coy HQrs & Supply Section moved to billets at TEMPLOUX	(MC)
VEZIN	19/12/18	—	Fair. Coy HQrs & Supply Section moved to billets at VEZIN	(MC)
HUY	20/12/18	—	Fair. Coy HQrs moved to billets at HUY Inquiries	(MC)

WAR DIARY
or
INTELLIGENCE SUMMARY
(Erase heading not required.)

Army Form C. 2118.

Place	Date	Hour	Summary of Events and Information	Remarks and references to Appendices
HQ Cairo	20/12/17	—	Weather fine. Usual Routine	C/HC
—	21/12/17	—	do do do	C/HC
—	22/12/17	—	do do S/4/070398 Pte Baxter CHM I admitted T/4/057450 Dr Shepton LE } 140 FJA	C/HC
—	23/12/17	—	do Supplies now drawn from HVS Arsenal by HT. Refilling Stock Place at 11-30	C/HC
—	24/12/17	—	do do Usual Routine	C/HC
—	25/12/17	—	do do T/4/057450 Dr Shepton LE returned to duty from 140 d FA	C/HC
—	26/12/17	—	do do Usual Routine	C/HC
—	27/12/17	—	Wet do T/4/250123 Cpl Stay E Successful in T/3/017016 Dr Jagler M demobilising T/4/057681 Dr Osborn J	C/HC
—	28/12/17	—	do Wet Usual Routine T/5/176.8 M/P Beeley JA admitted 140 d FA	C/HC
—	29/12/17	—	do do Usual Routine	C/HC

WAR DIARY
or
INTELLIGENCE SUMMARY.

Army Form C. 2118.

(Erase heading not required.)

Place	Date	Hour	Summary of Events and Information	Remarks and references to Appendices
H.V.S.	30/12/18		Weather fair. Normal Routine. S/Sgt 072338 Pte Bowker C.H.M. returned to duty from U.C. & F.A. Only H.Q. 7 O.R. Churchgoers & attended off the string the Newel Bradrie	(over)
	31/12/18		Weather wet.	(over)

C.H. Lyons
Capt. R.A.S.C.
OC. H. Coy 41st S. Div't Train

WAR DIARY
or
INTELLIGENCE SUMMARY.
(Erase heading not required.)

Army Form C. 2118.

NO 4 COY

Place	Date	Hour	Summary of Events and Information	Remarks and references to Appendices
HQ	1/7	—	Weather fine	
			Normal Routine	
			T/36130 Pte Morley W.H. proceeded to England for	
			Umit Duty.	(HC
—	2/7	—	do	Normal Routine. Supply by wagon of 11th ATA	(HC
			found they went for attd Command	
—	3/7	—	do	Normal Routine	(HC
—	4/7	—	do	do	T/423506 Pte Fullman B	
			T/166193 Pte Liphill P	
			T/068089 Pte Lillwood H	
			T/10184 Pte Harrell J	(HC
—	5/7	—	do	Normal Routine. Two Rifles took	
			place for completion of list	
			Baggage & wagon Train sent for Harwood	(HC
			Third to three men	
—	6/7	—	do	Supply by Wagon found rests for 2nd & 4th	(HC

Army Form C. 2118.

WAR DIARY
or
INTELLIGENCE SUMMARY.
(Erase heading not required.)

Instructions regarding War Diaries and Intelligence Summaries are contained in F. S. Regs., Part II. and the Staff Manual respectively. Title pages will be prepared in manuscript.

Place	Date	Hour	Summary of Events and Information	Remarks and references to Appendices
On TRAIN	7/9		Weather fine. Cy Headquarters train arrived at ANDENNES at 13 hours. No showers. Supply wagon & baggage wagon travelled by self with the Major outside. Supply wagon 11th R.F.A were handed over at HUY to the Cy. Jr Caradoc 51st Group. Supply wagons to the dift Middlesex & 52nd M.V.S. 15/1 Cy. sent to Brd. 19 9200.	Che
HEUMAR	8/9	do	German train arrived at 2 hours. Cy. detrained at BEASBURG at 11 hours & marched to billets at HEUMAR. Supplies delivered 15 Cy. M.T.	Che
—	9/9	do	Regions delivered by M.T. Return for Brigade. Battalions delivered by M.T. Returns for langue de Vaches	Che
—	10/9	do	The usual Returns. Baggage & Supply wagons informed by Train service	Che
—	11/9	do	The usual Returns	Che
—	12/9	do	do. Supply wagon 138th F.A. forward for further orders	Che

(A9175) Wt W2358/P360 60,000 17/7 D. D. & L. Sch. 52a. Forms/C2118/13

Army Form C. 2118

WAR DIARY
or
INTELLIGENCE SUMMARY
(Erase heading not required.)

Instructions regarding War Diaries and Intelligence Summaries are contained in F.S. Regs., Part II. and the Staff Manual respectively. Title Pages will be prepared in manuscript.

Place	Date	Hour	Weather	Summary of Events and Information	Remarks and references to Appendices
HEUMAR	13/5/9				[illegible]
—	14/5/9			Stepf. Inv. known from ROSRATH confirmed by H.T. T/4/24423 to Wright R.M. from from GHQ S.C. been sufferd	[illegible]
—	15/5/9			Manual Raubitz Staff of Major 228 F.C. R.E/ready for attached	[illegible]
—	16/5/9			do T/1/10184 St Farrell J. admitted 140 F.A.	[illegible]
—	17/5/9			do	[illegible]
—	18/5/9			do	[illegible]
—	19/5/9			do T/1/10184 St Farrell J. returned to duty from 139 F.A.	[illegible]
—	20/5/9			do T/4/088059 to Sullivan M. In agreement to T/4244223 St Wright R.M. since and by Royle Hdqs	[illegible]
—	21/5/9			do Manual Routine	[illegible]
—	22/5/9			do Manual Routine	[illegible]
—	23/5/9			do do	[illegible]

Army Form C. 2118

WAR DIARY
or
INTELLIGENCE SUMMARY
(Erase heading not required.)

Instructions regarding War Diaries and Intelligence Summaries are contained in F.S. Regs., Part II. and the Staff Manual respectively. Title Pages will be prepared in manuscript.

Place	Date	Hour	Summary of Events and Information	Remarks and references to Appendices
HEUMAR	24/5	—	Marched from A/553 & Wilhelm L.J. proceeded to England for demobilization	(Inc)
—	25/5	—	do	(Inc)
—	26/5	—	No filling of oil had any to new area west of [?]	(Inc)
—	27/5	—	Supply by lorry. Filling took place at HEUMAR railhead at 9.00 hours. Supply wagons 228 F.C. R.E. joined	(Inc)
—	28/5	—	do. No 2 Coy 4/0/5 Army Filling at HEUMAR railhead at 8.00	(Inc)
—	29/5	—	do. No filling at Rail[?]	(Inc)
—	30/5	—	do. do	(Inc)
—	31/5	—	do. do	(Inc)

[signature] Capt R.A.S.C.
O.C. 4 Coy 4/0 Divisional Train

WAR DIARY

or
INTELLIGENCE SUMMARY

(Erase heading not required.)

Army Form C. 2118

Place	Date	Hour	Summary of Events and Information	Remarks and references to Appendices
HEUMAR	1 2/5		Weather fine. Move Routine.	(re
—	2 2/5		do. Brig.r. Major on of 10th Queen's & 20th St L. Joined staff unity. Sgt. of H.Q. of H.Q.	(re
—	3 2/5		do. moved Routine. Brig. of 2pn rttn Rink	(re
—	4 2/5		do.	(re
—	5 2/5		do.	(re
—	6 2/5		do.	(re
—	7 2/5		do. Capt. E.S. Mudham R.M.S.C. transferred to advance H.T. dep. at 9 o'clock. He also attended	(re
—	8 2/5		do. Staff of Major sent signals CR E. 12 Bn M/S a 5th Q of sent no 1 of signals Major — 12 b. Bty. R.F.A. were not attached. Lt. 1. 158, 70 Actg Cpl Penny Inf. to life Tu 1/12 373 to Johnson Jnr Rfm. to life TU 1/686 595 Rfm. a Achuntted into L.J.A.	(re

WAR DIARY
or
INTELLIGENCE SUMMARY
(Erase heading not required.)

Army Form C. 2118

Place	Date	Hour	Summary of Events and Information	Remarks and references to Appendices
HEVMAR	9/2/19	Weather Fine	Ment Rates 201663 Pts Jackson W.J. 2538th Employment of Churchyard of Cemetery etc.	(see)
	10/2/19	Weather Fine	Ment Ranton	(see)
	11/2/19	Weather Fine	Ment Ranton No 74/086395 to Jason A returned to duty from 140th Field Ambulance	(see)
	12/2/19	Weather Fine	do T/34122 to Walsh J.J. travel & taken on the strength of from 1/46 L.F.A.	(see)
	13/2/19	Weather Fine	do	(see)
	14/2/19	Weather Fine	do No 201619 Pte Mallock forwarded to 238th Employment Coy for demobilization	(see)
	15/2/19	Weather Fine	do	(see)
	16/2/19	Weather Fine	do T4/060725 A/Sgt Stockney M. struck off strength from 15/19 on having attained age 308555 Pte Caudle S.L. 238th Employment Coy forwarded for demob also T/403359 Pte Hogg J. returned to duty from 140 S/F.A	(see)

WAR DIARY
or
INTELLIGENCE SUMMARY
(Erase heading not required.)

Army Form C. 2118

Place	Date	Hour	Summary of Events and Information	Remarks and references to Appendices
HEVMAR	17th		Weather wet. Normal Routine. Relieved No. TS/7/685 L/Cpl Jennerson H admitted 140 1t FA	(over)
	18d		Weather wet. Normal Routine. [illegible] Nos. 30,853 Pte Grumer S., 607, 679 Maddox L.	(over)
	19th		Weather dull. do.	(over)
	20th		Weather wet. do. Nos. TS/9149 Saddler L/Cpl Patrick CE, S/31409b Pte Evans JH	(over)
	21st		Weather fine. do.	(over) (over)
	22nd		do.	(over)
	23rd		do.	(over)
	24d		do.	(over)
	25th		do. 2 Bdy WO3 and 2 supply Wagon proceeded to [illegible]	
	26th		do. Nos 15678 Pte [illegible] B, 238 Employment Coy Posted off the strength	(over)

WAR DIARY
or
INTELLIGENCE SUMMARY
(Erase heading not required.)

Army Form C. 2118

Place	Date	Hour	Summary of Events and Information	Remarks and references to Appendices
HEUMAR	27th		Weather fine. Usual Routine	(K)(sd) (C)(sd)
	28th		do	

Signature
O.C. 4 Coy [illegible]

Army Form C. 2118.

WAR DIARY
or
INTELLIGENCE SUMMARY.
(Erase heading not required.)

Instructions regarding War Diaries and Intelligence Summaries are contained in F. S. Regs., Part II. and the Staff Manual respectively. Title pages will be prepared in manuscript.

Place	Date	Hour	Summary of Events and Information	Remarks and references to Appendices
HEUVAR	1/3/19		Weather fine. Named Rawlins, one N.D. Batty in charge this unit detached to 26th Battn D.L.I. photograph 28/2/19. 2 Baggage & 2 Supply Wagons were handed over to 26th Battn D.L.I. on leaving. 141st Brigade 2 Baggage & 2 Supply Wagons were received from Bn 3rd Battn Regt [illegible] ... on joining the 2nd Bde.	
—	2/3/19		Weather fine	(Inc)
—	3/3/19		Weather wet	(Inc)
—	4/3/19		Weather wet	(Inc)
—	5/3/19		Weather fine	(Inc)
—	6/3/19		Weather fine	(Inc)
—	7/3/19		Weather fine	(Inc)
—	8/3/19		Weather fine. No S4/058848 Pte Graham W admitted 140th F.A.	(Inc)
—	9/3/19		Weather fine. 1 Rider Cpl and 3 Pte struck off strength & struck off strength to T5/9619 Cpl Michel J.G. Raleigh J. returned to [illegible]	

WAR DIARY
or
INTELLIGENCE SUMMARY.

(Erase heading not required.)

Army Form C. 2118.

Place	Date	Hour	Summary of Events and Information	Remarks and references to Appendices
HEVMAR	9th Jan 18		Duty from 140 & F.A. T4/059720 St Sheasby	
	10 3/18		Weather fair and fine	
	11 3/18		" fine	
	12 3/18		" fine	
	13 3/18		" fine. On H.Q. Cy Rolls died.	
	14 3/18		" fine T3/7619 Wheelwright Raleigh J. admitted 140 & F.A.	
			S/O 50948 Pte Graham M. returned to duty from 140 & F.A. & M.S.	
	15 3/18		Weather fine On H.Q. 44 wounded	
	16 3/18		" fine do	
	17 3/18		Weather dull snow T4/059770 St Sheasby J returned to duty.	
	18 3/18		Weather fine Duty from 140 F.A.	
			T3/026997 Cpl Watson A. admitted	
			140 F.A.	
	19 3/18		Weather fine Two H.D. Nos 48 & 170 letter from no. 7 Cy	
			to white clay Crystalline Amyl Nor	
			sending. To F known	

WAR DIARY
or
INTELLIGENCE SUMMARY

Army Form C. 2118.

Place	Date	Hour	Summary of Events and Information	Remarks and references to Appendices
HEUMAR	20/3/19		Weather fine. Normal Routine	(WC
	21/3/19		do	15/1/19 Fr. Wheeler Raleigh returned to Unity from 140 & FA	(WC
				Pre H.D & 1 mule received from Reserve Collection Camp	
				Pre H.D. Cy 70 to the administrat'n of 57 H.VS	
	22/3/19		do		(WC
	23/3/19		do	13/02/6/9/9 M.H. Watson A returned to duty from 140 & FA. 2 H.D. Cy nos 41/9, 132, 9/4, L.D by no 8, 1 mule Cy no 54. 15 anemal Collection Camp	(WC
	24/3/19		do	Two H.D Cys nos 41.9.32 were returned from anmal Collection Camp nos 9/15	(WC
				5 class of animal offered my Johari ??.	
	25/3/19		do	Pre L.D & 1 mule returned from anmal Collection Camp	(WC

Army Form C. 2118.

WAR DIARY
or
INTELLIGENCE SUMMARY.
(Erase heading not required.)

Place	Date	Hour	Summary of Events and Information	Remarks and references to Appendices
HEUMAR	25/9/18		A/E 1898 Sgt [illeg] S.G. } Proceeded to Command Station	A/c
			T/58/02798 Cpl Hayward H.L. } Camp for demobilization	
			T4/049420 Sgt Brown C.H. }	
	26/9		Weather Wet Moved Routine	A/c
	27/9		do Bad do	A/c
	28/9		do Wet do	A/c
	29/9		do do do	A/c
	30/9		do Snow do	A/c
	31/9		do Snow Supply Wagons A.T.C. Battery	A/c
			to G.H. Bgh A.F.A. handed off to	
			Officers others made	
			[signature] Capt	
			OC H By [illeg] Bn [illeg]	

WAR DIARY
INTELLIGENCE SUMMARY

Army Form C. 2118.

Place	Date	Hour	Summary of Events and Information	Remarks and references to Appendices
Kermann	1/7/19		Weather wet - Usual Routine	J.C.
"	2/7/19		Weather fine Usual Routine	J.C.
"	3/7/19		Weather fine Usual Routine	J.C.
"	4/7/19	Fine	2 I.D. Horses nos 41 & 32 sent to D.A.R.C.	WSM
"	5/7/19	"	6 I.D. Horses received from D.A.R.C. 6 off. & 6. belonging R.A.S.C.	WSM
"	6/7/19	Fine	4 Lianopings to " Sail train " left W to hail R.A.S.C. from Lodge. London quiet rain. 1 I.D. Horse no. 141 returned from D.A.R.C.	WSM
"	7/7/19	"	1 Ridg drawn for No. 8 Company train.	WSM
"	8/7/19	Fair	1 I.D. Horse drawn from D.A.R.C.	WSM
"	9/7/19	Fair	Usual Routine. Lieut. J. Cavanagh R.A.S.C. transferred to Scotland. Quiet rain.	WSM
"	10/7/19	"	do.	WSM
"	11/7/19	"	do.	WSM
"	12/7/19	Wet	do.	WSM
"	13/7/19	Fair	do.	WSM
"	14/7/19	"	do.	WSM
"	15/7/19	"	do.	WSM
"	16/7/19	Wet	do. T/4/088059. Pte Jallaize W rejoined from 3rd London Brigade Todgis.	WSM

WAR DIARY
or
INTELLIGENCE SUMMARY.

(Erase heading not required.)

Army Form C. 2118.

Place	Date	Hour	Summary of Events and Information	Remarks and references to Appendices
FIENVILLERS	14/4/19		Weather fair. Usual Routine. T/1/080949 S/Sgt Whitlow & T/4/06193 Sadd to taken to T/404/7254 Sr Beat to T/41296. S/ Leigh Q. T/10769. Sr Lovell (B. joined from Guards Batt.	W.S.M.
	15/4/19		Train T/1411/3506, Sadd & field to Q Workshop & taken to admitted 140 J.A. Lieut. B.C. Russell. R.A.S.C. joined from 14th Dist. Train	W.S.M.
	16/4/19		T/300193 Sr Leslie to joined from Guards Div: train. T/3033859 Sr Coogh	W.S.M.
	19/4/19		Transferred to 34th London Bde: Coys.	W.S.M.
	20/4/19	do.		W.S.M.
	21/4/19	do.		W.S.M.
	22/4/19	do.	T/421401. Sr Vincent transferred to 20 D. Div: train	W.S.M.
	23/4/19	do.	T/138561. Sr Lowell to joined from Guards Div: train	W.S.M.
	24/4/19	do.	Coy transport vehicles transferred to G.O.C. Division	W.S.M.
	25/4/19	do.		W.S.M.
	26/4/19	do.	ET/41/816 Sr Heritage & to proceeded for demobilization do T/4/21524/4	W.S.M.
	27/4/19	do.	Sr Smith to joined from 20 Div: train	W.S.M.
	28/4/19	do.	T/7384921 Sr Lowell to T/309193 Sr Leslie to transferred to 140 J.A.	W.S.M.
	29/4/19	do.	do.	W.S.M.
	30/4/19	do.	T/4/43066 Sadd to both to W.Agoinval for duty from 140 J.A.	W.S.M.

W.S. Maile
CAPT. O.C. No. 1 COMPANY
LONDON DIVISIONAL TRAIN R.A.S.C.

WAR DIARY
or
INTELLIGENCE SUMMARY.

(Erase heading not required.)

Army Form C. 2118.

Place	Date	Hour	Summary of Events and Information	Remarks and references to Appendices
HEUMAR	1/9/19		Usual Routine.	wsm
"	2/9/19		Do. No Ty/18586 Dr Law Burns R. joined from 20th	wsm
			Field Amb:	
"	3/9/19		Usual Routine. No Ty/18547 Dr Smith to transferred to today's	wsm
			3rd London Inf. Bde.	
"	4/9/19		Do.	wsm
"	5/9/19		Do. No T/305405 Dr. Ira Gregory admitted 140 Field Amb.	wsm
			Taf/8643 Dr. Connell joined from 14th Dist. Lan	
"	6/9/19		Do. No Ty/08050 Dr Jakeys Wr returned to duty from	
			140th Field Amb. 1 Rider Class B1. joined from 14 Dist. Lan	
			1 Rider Class B1. transferred from today's London Dist. Lan	
			Taf/12446. Dr. Kerr A.G. } joined from 14th Army Anne (H) By.	wsm
			T/305346 " Brown A. G.	
			T/342396 " Connon A.B.	
"	7/9/19		Usual Routine. T/305405 Dr Ira Gregory, evacuated to	wsm
			No 64 6.6.6.	

WAR DIARY
or
INTELLIGENCE SUMMARY.
(Erase heading not required.)

Army Form C. 2118.

Place	Date	Hour	Summary of Events and Information	Remarks and references to Appendices
HEUMAR	8/9		Heavy Routine.	
			2/Lt Pollard. Dr. Labours W.	
			T/Lieut 540505 . Soulby J.	
			13/026079 . Whale J.	
			4/4290 . Whittle J. } Transferred to 4th Army Arra (H) Bn	wdy
			T/4344774. Lt. White G.	
			T/404554 . G. Rook B.	
			T/4054460 . Buttler C.V.	
			1/35633 . Taylor W.B.	
			13/10/69 . Russel B.	
			T/402505. Pte (A/Sgt) Dugsdale I. joined from 14th Army Area (H)Bn.	wdm
		9/9	Heavy Routine.	
			Do.	
		10/9	Do. No. T/36555 Pt. Lord C.V. returned to duty from 64 C.C.S.	
			No T/4459 W.O. II. Sgt Buert L.G. } Proceeded to U.K. for demobilization & struck off strength.	Wth
			T/4000696. Dr. Smith C.B.	
			T/4084 . Round J.	
			T/4452113. Worrsford E.R.	

WAR DIARY
or
INTELLIGENCE SUMMARY.
(Erase heading not required.)

Army Form C. 2118.

Place	Date	Hour	Summary of Events and Information	Remarks and references to Appendices
HEUMAR	11/5/19	—	Usual Routine. 1st D. Coms No 1052 Class B/V destroyed 6.3.19. and struck off strength.	WWm
"	12/5/19	"	Usual Routine. Baggage trucks join units for Brigade move.	WWm
ROSRATH	13/5/19	"	Coy Colors & Buffs Section move to Rosrath and take over billets confined to hq. & Coy. and also Buffs. Baggage wagons & Units remaining in forward area.	WWm
"	14/5/19	"	Usual Routine.	WWm
"	15/5/19	"	Do. T/320091 Dr PERRY S.W. wounded to U.K. for	WWm
"	16/5/19	"	rehabilitation and struck off the strength. Usual Routine. T/4055370 Dr (A/cpl) BARRY (H.) T/4161124 Dr MONTHEY (J.) proceeded to U.K. for demobilization T/4055920 Dr DANDLIN (J.) and struck off the strength. T/241122 " WALSH (K.) T/326161 Dr HAZLE R. joined from 14th Army Auxy (H) Coy and taken on the strength.	Wlly

WAR DIARY
or
INTELLIGENCE SUMMARY.

(Erase heading not required.)

Army Form C. 2118.

Place	Date	Hour	Summary of Events and Information	Remarks and references to Appendices
BASRAH.	14/5/19		Weather fine. Usual Routine.	WM
"	18/5/19		do.	WM
"	19/5/19		do. Hosbn Lt Taylor L. 6/58th Employment Coy returned to Unit – struck off strength.	WM
"	20/5/19		do.	WM
"	21/5/19		do. Coy ("D" Coy hitherto "AY") surrendered to 52nd S.Y.S.	WM
"	22/5/19		do. struck off strength	WM
"	23/5/19		do.	WM
"	24/5/19		do.	WM
"	25/5/19		do.	WM
"	26/5/19		do. 7/42. D. Sattan J.Ko. ⎫ proceeded to U.K. for demobilization 23/5/19 and struck off the strength	
			7/39624H – Parker Ko. ⎬	
			7/30/9051 – Sabori ( )	
			7/36169 – Walker ( )	
			7/9/10di D. Saunders (?) joined from 4th Army Group (?) Coy.	
			Sepoy Lt. Leuthorpe D.B. struck off strength of diary as such. L.R.O. No.2496, dated 22.5/19.	WM

WAR DIARY
or
INTELLIGENCE SUMMARY.
(Erase heading not required.)

Army Form C. 2118.

Place	Date	Hour	Summary of Events and Information	Remarks and references to Appendices
RATH	27/9	—	Weather fine. "Usual Routine". No 105404 A/Sgt Burdell D. 238th Employment - Coy joined and taken on strength.	
"	28/9	—	No 71/28434 Gnr Brown A.W. joined from No 2 Company.	WWH
"	29/9	—	fine. Usual Routine. No 104451 Dvr Walker J. & Gnr from 238th Employment	WWH
"	30/9	—	fine. Usual Routine. Coy 28.5.19.	WWH
"	1/9	—	" Do.	WWH
"	2/9	—	" Do.	WWH

Capt

WAR DIARY
or
INTELLIGENCE SUMMARY.
(Erase heading not required.)

Army Form C. 2118.

Place	Date	Hour	Summary of Events and Information	Remarks and references to Appendices
Aisne	1/9		Weather fine. Usual Routine	
"	2/9		" T/086895 S/Sgt Luvin A. T/57608 M/S Perebv. L.C. proceeded to U.K. for demobilisation	G/W/D
"			T/026996 - Paine T. T/313446 S/Cutler R.D.	G/W/D
"			T/4/211434 Cpl Perry B. appointed Sergeant authority R.A.S.D.	
"			T/060908 S/Sergeant W. " L/Cpl. Lancs L/cpl a/v Ag 31/9	
"	3/9		Usual Routine. 2/Lieut R.C. Russell to No 36	G/W/D
"			2/Lieut R.D. Mayson to No 4 Coy. 2/Lieut to No 1 Coy.	
"			T/40923 S/Cary M.C. rejoined from M.T. Company	
"	4/9		Usual Routine. T/386427 S/Haviland C. joined Coy from 17 Gen Hosp	G/W/D
"			432704 Pte Darke W.J. " " 15 "	
"	5/9		" T/083062 A/Sgt Baysdale T. posted to No 2. Compy.	G/W/D
"	6/9		" T/12373 Pte Inglow J.W. appointed Corpl.	G/W/D
"	7/9		" T/110334 S/ Burling J. " Cpl.	G/W/D
"			T/510248 " Copley J " S/Sgt	G/W/D
"			T/260135 " Corp. Marshall J " Stan Sgt	G/W/D
"			T/143046 " Sadr. Noble H.W. " Sect. Cpl.	

Army Form C. 2118.

WAR DIARY
or
INTELLIGENCE SUMMARY.
(Erase heading not required.)

Instructions regarding War Diaries and Intelligence Summaries are contained in F.S. Regs., Part II. and the Staff Manual respectively. Title pages will be prepared in manuscript.

Place	Date	Hour	Summary of Events and Information	Remarks and references to Appendices
Recreat	8/5/19		Weather fine. Usual Routine. T/3/026997 Cpl Moton. A. T/3/7383 Sar. Cpl. Milton. E.	Received 8/WD
"	9/5/19		T/S/9685 Md. Cpl. Gemenson H. S/025843 Pte Gordon. W	for demobilization 8/WD
			T/4/206195. Sad. Sr Graham. H	
			632285. Pte. Fuller. J.H. 652226 Pte Maulbey. J. Joined C from 238 Sup. C.	6/WD
"	10/5/19		Changeable " " I.H.D. 6. No.4 C.	6/WD
"	11/5/19		Raining " "	6/WD
"	12/5/19		Thunder " "	6/WD
"	13/5/19		Changeable " "	6/WD
"	14/5/19		Fine " " I.L.D from 52. M.V.S.	6/WD
			4016228. Cpl Clark. A. } Proceeded to U.K.	
			14/38906 S. Tullgamer. S. } for	
			T/3/026930 Cpl. Beamon. W } demobilization	
"	15/5/19		Fine 1	2/WD
"	16/5/19		" "	6/WD
"	17/5/19		" Lt. Battn O.H. joining C. 2/Lt. Clark & Pte. Atkinson. from 26 R.E.	6/WD
"	18/5/19		"	6/WD
"	19/5/19		" Company move to Oresat.	6/WD

WAR DIARY
or
INTELLIGENCE SUMMARY.
(Erase heading not required.)

Army Form C. 2118.

Instructions regarding War Diaries and Intelligence Summaries are contained in F. S. Regs., Part II. and the Staff Manual respectively. Title pages will be prepared in manuscript.

Place	Date	Hour	Summary of Events and Information	Remarks and references to Appendices
Moascar	20/9		Weather fine. Normal Routine. Erected Tents. Cross lines s.l.	6/W.D
"	21/9		"	6/W.D
"	22/9		"	6/W.D
"	23/9		" Raining Pte. Cooper, J.A. joined Co. from No.1. Co.	6/W.D
"	24/9		" Pte. Carroll J.M. 1st Ellis } attached to	6/W.D
			" Pte. Ellis J. " } 15	
			" Pte. Brown C.M, 11th Queens } Company.	
"	25/9		" Changeable Young G.H. 10th Queens attached	6/W.D
			" Parker, N 26. R.F } to	
			" Meade H.R.1. 19. Ellis } Company.	
			" B.L. M. 23 "	
"	26/9		" Rain Stormy L.Cpll Lee. & Pte. Kerr. transferred to 3rd Lon. Inf. Bge.	6/W.D
"	27/9		" " Cpl. Rushing admitted Hospital	6/W.D
			" " Sgt. Tophin, Pte Barker } proceeded to U.K.	
			" " Pte. Talbot. 1/C. Buttle C/S } for Demobilization	
"	28	5pm.	" Opening of Peace terms read out to Company.	6/W.D

(A9475) Wt W2353/P360 600,000 12/17 D. D. & L. Sch. 82u Form/C2118/15.

Army Form C. 2118.

WAR DIARY
or
INTELLIGENCE SUMMARY.
(Erase heading not required.)

Instructions regarding War Diaries and Intelligence Summaries are contained in F. S. Regs., Part II. and the Staff Manual respectively. Title pages will be prepared in manuscript.

Place	Date	Hour	Summary of Events and Information	Remarks and references to Appendices
Cooperal	29/9		Weather Rain Stormy Usual Routine	6/11/19
"	30/9		" Capt M.S. Marks, leave to U.K. Lt. B. Baget, attached to Cpom 11/16.	6/11/19

E. Baget
CAPT.
O. C. "J" COMPANY
LONDON DIVISIONAL ... R. S. C.

WAR DIARY or INTELLIGENCE SUMMARY.

(Erase heading not required.)

Army Form C. 2118.

Place	Date	Hour	Summary of Events and Information	Remarks and references to Appendices
ROSRATH	1/1/19	—	Weather fine. Lieut. Gerath 4:30 a.m. arrived Rosrath E.O. am.	
"	2/1/19	"	Manual Routine. Lecture by Major Raynes on Was Savings Certificates	Weather too frosty.
"	3/1/19	"	Raining " 1. Rider G. No 2.C. 2 May 4 Hd 2 on return from M.P.F.	
"	4/1/19	"	Fine " 1. Rider, 4. Hd, 2. May. 1. Sgt. r. 3. Ptes returned to No. 1. C.	
"	5/1/19	"	" 5" Pte Raleigh to Neuheim Camp for demobilisation Company Pay. Troop C.A.M.S. Baylor F. transferred to Supply Section. Col. Pershing J. discharged from Hospital.	
"	6/1/19	"	"	
"	7/1/19	"	" Pte. Moulton J.J. Pte. Malley Pte Hare Pte Clissitt Leave to U.K. 26/12/19 7.32704 Cpl. Dods. N.Z. to a/sgt with pay. T/1624 Pte. Gnr. Pratt A.L.C. Mt. Blanch Bay (transfere from Mt. 1.B) Pte Clarke D.A.C. returned to Units.	U.K. 26/12/19 R.M Pte Wardes al. 13 day Pay F.P. no 2
"	8/1/19	"	" Pte. Edgar. C. carpenter 28 days F.P. No 2 Pte Wardes al. 13 day pay F.P. no 2 1. F.S. Loader, 2. Hd, 1 May returned to No. 1. C. 1. H.Q. Boy Geld to 52 Wollotte Sch. Seshen.	
"	9/1/19	"	Cloudy "	

Army Form C. 2118.

WAR DIARY
or
INTELLIGENCE SUMMARY.
(Erase heading not required.)

Instructions regarding War Diaries and Intelligence Summaries are contained in F.S. Regs., Part II. and the Staff Manual respectively. Title pages will be prepared in manuscript.

Place	Date	Hour	Summary of Events and Information	Remarks and references to Appendices
Boscat	10/7/19	—	Weather, Raining. Naval Ratings 52/5023 Skipper St Leod P.M. transferred from No 2 Coy. Pte Edgar E. to Field Punishment Barracks, Bologne	
"	11/7/19	"	Changeable. Removed from Lui to Faren.	
"	12/7/19	"	Raining.	
"	13/7/19	"	Changeable. 1st Pnyr. L.B. 3rd Pnyr. H.D. Shaw at Hammer.	
"	14/7/19	2 "	Raining. T/7672 M.S. Sgt. Barons, O. transferred from No 1 Co T/7624 " " Pratt, A.E. " to No 1 Co	
"	15/7/19	" "	Changeable. Lt/ Balahni. Op/ Capt. 235. Sup to returned to 1st Reserve. Lieut J. Steward. reported from Law, U.K.	
"	16/7/19	"	Fine. T/C 29127 J. Heath. E.J. demobilized U.K. 29/7/19 Capt. Allen, Lee Part 15y 9/7/19 4.7.19 Pte Cooper, F. (Baker) Returns to No 1 Co.	
"	17/7/19	"	VI. Corps Shaw 2nd Pnyr. H.D. VI R.E. Baggage returned to L.	
"	18/7/19	"	Meeting all officers at Hotel Hammer, 12.00. Company Coy Sgt Bodley, R.F. born to U.K. 9/7/19 6.2/19. Lieut Bryer J. attended to No 1 Co	
"	19/7/19	"	T/32709 Sgt Death, W.F. transferred to 140 Field Ambulance T/10354 Cpl Burling J. appointed Sgt (Residence Pay)	

Army Form C. 2118.

WAR DIARY
or
INTELLIGENCE SUMMARY.
(Erase heading not required.)

Instructions regarding War Diaries and Intelligence Summaries are contained in F. S. Regs., Part II. and the Staff Manual respectively. Title pages will be prepared in manuscript.

Place	Date	Hour	Summary of Events and Information	Remarks and references to Appendices
Rouen	20/1/19	—	Weather Raining. General Routine. T/392416 S/Sgr. A. admitted 11th Stat. (Capt. M.S. Watt return from leave)	
"	21/1/19	"	" Pte. Page J. awarded 14 days F.P. No.2 attached from No.3.L	
"	22/1/19	"	Cloudy. Capt. W.J. White to No.1. Company. (Pte. Overbury C.A. 7 days C.C.)	
"	23/1/19	"	Raining. T/110.334. A/Sgt. Burleigh J. Posted to 139 Field Ambulance as Relieve Paymaster to Imperial Matters.	
"	24/1/19	"	Fine	
"	25/1/19	"	"	
"	26/1/19	"	" T/392416 S/Sgr. A. Discharged Hospital.	
"	27/1/19	"	"	
"	28/1/19	"	" T/327396. S/Lieut. A. admitted Hospital (Lees Relating returned) Lieut. J.S. Steward. Officer Commanding No.3 Coy (Capt M. Mait) attended examination of shipping transferring to R.A.S.C.	
"	29/1/19	"	"	
"	30/1/19	"	" 579905. Pte. Cooper J. Cove E. O.K. 30/7 5-13/7/5	
"	31/1/19	"	" Company Pay. Typewriter returned to T.H.Q. 24. Infantry Divisib transferred to R.A.S.C. (W. Company).	

CAPT. O.C. No. 4 COMPANY
LONDON DIVISIONAL TRAIN R.A.S.C.

WAR DIARY or INTELLIGENCE SUMMARY

Army Form C. 2118.

Place	Date	Hour	Summary of Events and Information	Remarks and references to Appendices
Roverto	1/7/19	—	Weather fine. Heavy rain. 151520. Pte. Freeman. H.J. Admitted Hosp.	
"	2/7/19	—	Lt. Lennan. A. Sev. Lieut. Tobruk gel wichelsey St. appointed. E.Q.M.S. aut. R.A.O.C. arr. 30/9/19 5/7/19 Pte. Edgar. E.T. Pte. Page. T.T. Moved Palestine.	
"	3/7/19	"	Mth. P. Baker. Leave U.K. 5/7/19 6/19/19. Sgt. Beddy 24/7/19.	
"	4/7/19	"	Pte. Ellington A to 26. R.E. details	
"	~~5/7/19~~	"	St. Conner returned to Unit from Washment	
"	5/7/19	"	Lt. Coventry. F.A. Leave U.K. 6/7/19 15/20/19.	
"	"	"	Pte. Vaughan " 6/7/19 to 20/7/19	
"	6/7/19	"	Lt. Byens. C.T. Pte. Sutton. F. Pte. Ellis. Pleave U.K. 6/7/19 6/21/19. Pte. Paddock, Pte. Gregson, Pte. Ptr. Valley. " 7/7/19 6/22/19 Lt. Loman. A. Leave U.K. 7/7/19 6/21/19.	
"	7/7/19	"	Horses Blacksmith by Board. Pte. Lt. Lt. Parsons. Leave. U.K. 7/7/19 6/21/19 Sadd. Sgt. North.	

WAR DIARY
or
INTELLIGENCE SUMMARY.

Army Form C. 2118.

Place	Date	Hour	Summary of Events and Information	Remarks and references to Appendices
Rosrath	8/7/19		Weather fine. Usual routine. Pte Albery L + Pte Payne S. Cornwall Leave U.K. 9/7/19 6. 23/7/19	
	9/7/19		Pte Whiting E. returned from leave. 15 days absent. Pte Carter P.E. + Pte Brown A.W. Leave U.K. 10/7/19 6. 24/7/19	
	10/7/19		C.Q.M. Mulcahy C.F. reported to No. 2 Co. for duty. Pte Chudd F. Transferred to No. 3 Company	
	"		Pte Foster J. + Pte Fisher Leave U.K. 11/7/19 6. 25/7/19	
	"		Pte Moulton J.J. 23t Sup. Co. to U.K. for dismount{dem}	
	11/7/19		Cpl Payne F, Pte Carroll M. 17 R.F. Leave U.K. 12/7/19 6. 26/7/19	
	"		C.S.M. Mulcahy C.F. transferred to No. 2 Company	
Köln	12/7/19		Company removed to New Camp. "East Köln"	
	"		Farr. Sgt Marschall J.M. to No. 2 Company for duty.	
	"		Sadd. St. Crewe C.W. + Pte Christmas E. Leave U.K. 13/7/19 6. 27/7/19	
	13/7/19			
	14/7/19		Pte Edgar C. Pte Page T.T. 5 days C.B. St Grant P. 3 days C.B. Company Pay. Pte Davis J.J. + Pte Walker V.C. Leave U.K. 15/7/19 6. 29/7/19	

Army Form C. 2118.

WAR DIARY
or
INTELLIGENCE SUMMARY.
(Erase heading not required.)

Instructions regarding War Diaries and Intelligence Summaries are contained in F.S. Regs., Part II. and the Staff Manual respectively. Title pages will be prepared in manuscript.

Place	Date	Hour	Summary of Events and Information	Remarks and references to Appendices
Buck.	16/7/19		Marker Line Naval Pavleed, T/o/S.R. 01405. C.S.M. Nightin, J. Transferred from No 3. Company 16 WO 4 Company T.R.O. Stay 11/1/15 - 3/1/19	
	16/7/19		Pte Ongu. J.T. St Lunt. awarded 7 days C.L.	
			Pte Dawson J. Pte Rackbury H. Spel Reynolds Rece U.K. 17/7/19 - 31/7/19	
	17/7/19		C.S.M. Nighton, J. reported for duty. Pte Cooper returned from leave.	
	18/7/19		Pte Allender. A. & Ayrer. J.M. Leave U.K. 19/7/19 - 2/8/19	
	19/7/19		Sgt. D. Lyon. U.K. 20/7/19 to 3/8/19 Pte Rondes K of C.Leave.	
	20/7/19		Cpl. A. Kerr U.K. 21/7/19 to 4/8/19	
			T/237373 Spl Jordan Jas. afgst 19.2.19	authority
			T/060705 Spl Swann W. apfrl 21.5.19	Phris Army
			T/453409 Spl Peek. G.A. Spl "	No. S.T/8/1/35
			T/453405 " Caron. R.S. Spl "	(F) 16.5.19
			T/453426 Bd J. Glennie J.U. " " Q.M. 10/5/19	
	21/7/19		S. Croutny, G.A. Pte Standfield, S. Baker. S. Returned from leave.	
			S. Croutry, G.A. & Pte Lane S. Baggage 1/R.F.	
			Pte Russell. J.M. returned to No 1. Company	

WAR DIARY
or
INTELLIGENCE SUMMARY.

Army Form C. 2118.

Place	Date	Hour	Summary of Events and Information	Remarks and references to Appendices
Kroon.	22/7/19		Weather fine. Usual Routine. S/Sgt Kelly H. & S/Lack T. leave U.K. 23/7/19 to 6.9/19.	
			Sgt. Colt. Returned from leave.	
	23/7/19		T.3/027006 S/ McGregor J. Surrendes to U.K. from Kergh.	
			S/ Packard Pte Ellis G. S/ Tetter S. Cryans proceed from leave U.K.	
			Mcl. S/ Sgt. Parsons.	
			S/ Freeman J. leave U.K. 24/7/19 to 7.9.19.	
	24/7/19	Raining	Sad. Mr Webb W.R, S/man A. Pte Kelly H. returned from leave.	
		"	Capt. J.C. Read reported for duty. S.O.	
			Pte S/George F. 235 Corp. B. returned from leave.	
			T.1/1015W S/Farrell J. arrested. Close arrest.	
	25/7/19	fine	S/ Cromwell J. returned from leave.	
		"	S/ McGregor J. shield H through 16/7/19 T.P.C. to 4/25/7.	
	26/7/19	Raining	T.1/1015W S/Farrell J. remanded F.G.C.M. (Closely Tried)	
			Pte Kelley R. & appeared J.Roy. Pay. 1 days pay R.W.	
			Pte Boyne P. S/ Faulkes J. S/ Feder R.A. returned from leave.	
			S/ Cooper P.L. Pte Bryson G.	

WAR DIARY
or
INTELLIGENCE SUMMARY
(Erase heading not required.)

Army Form C. 2118.

Place	Date	Hour	Summary of Events and Information	Remarks and references to Appendices
Neth.	27/9		Mechn. Inf. Lionel Peebles. Cpl. Swann W., L/Cpl. Pratt M. were U.K. 25/9 & 11/9.	
"			Pte. Porter, returned to MOI Company.	
"	28/9		Cpl. Payne F., & 17 R.F. returned from leave.	
"			Pte. Cassell J.M., St Christmas C.A., Sgt St Benson C.H. returned from leave U.K.	
"	29/9		L/H.D. on M.V.S. chief of charge.	
"			St Brown A.H. returned from leave U.K.	
"			Summary of Evidence St Farrell J. taken to E.H. Meeson, St Cooper R.S. expunged. 7 days Payp.	
"	30/9		Pte. Harris J.F., Pte. Mills W., returned from leave.	
"			Cpl. Kennon & Pte. Ewer, returned to 17 R.F.	
"	31/9		Pte. Philip J. returned to Unit. L/Cpl. Cornell, att from leave.	
"			T453000 Pte. Snell R.P., T/94605 St Saunders R. proceeded to	
"			No 1 Convalescent Camp for Demobilization	
"			St Lieut S. Page F.T. awarded 7 days R.E.	

CAPT. O. C. No. 4 COMPANY
LONDON DIVISIONAL TRAIN R.A.S.C

WAR DIARY or INTELLIGENCE SUMMARY

Army Form C. 2118.

Place	Date	Hour	Summary of Events and Information	Remarks and references to Appendices
Bach.	1. 1/1/19		Weather fine. Usual Routine. Lt Cornwell. G. and Lt Cash. N. detailed to 3.6. (Supply.)	
"	2. 2/1/19		Lt Stile. L.G. returned from leave U.K. (1 day absent) Lt Graham returned from U.K.	
"	3. 3/1/19		Lt Reed. A.T. Lt Fuller. J.H. leave U.K. 4/1/19 to 18/1/19	
"	4. 4/1/19		Pte. Saunders L. (26" R.F.) awarded 7 days. L.G. and returned to Unit	
"	"		" Meadow A. and Lt Ayres. G.M. returned from leave U.K.	
"	"		" Overa M. (admitted H.P.) with tonsilitis. St Pavis H.(adm H.P.)	
"	"		1/Lt R.W. Mayon, to Light Dut. Train.	
"	"		1/Lt F.E. Rennison from " { Auth: CR. ST. 14/149 (P) of/30.5.19.	
"	5. 5/1/19		MTZ. Lt Parker. S.C. attached 139. F.D. for assessing necessary Repairs to Wagon	
"	"		Pte. Holl. J. returned to Unit for Demobilisation. Pte. Jackson P.	
"	"		deprived 7 day's Pay/Compulsory Leave (U.K.) Pte. Topp A.M. returned from leave.	
"	6. 6/1/19		Blankets surrendered in accordance with G.R.O.	
"	"		1/Cpl. Payne, L. returned to Unit for Demobilisation.	
"	7. 7/1/19		Lt Melly R. and Lt Cash. N.T. returned from Leave. U.K.	
"	8. 8/1/19		Pte. O'Hara. D. (Sig H.P) Lt Andrews returned from leave.	
"	9. 9/1/19		Lt Paul. L.J. (adm H.P.) Pte Mayall returned to Unit for leave.	

Army Form C. 2118.

WAR DIARY
or
INTELLIGENCE SUMMARY.
(Erase heading not required.)

Instructions regarding War Diaries and Intelligence Summaries are contained in F. S. Regs., Part II. and the Staff Manual respectively. Title pages will be prepared in manuscript.

Place	Date	Hour	Summary of Events and Information	Remarks and references to Appendices
Shiel	11/9/19	Member Ino.	Usual Routine. Lt. Parr. A.R. Leave U.K. 11/9/19 to 25/9/19. Lt. Spelding to W.P.3. Company	
"	11/9/19	"	Lt. Pusi. W.J. discharged H.J. (Company Pay)	
"	12/9/19	"	L.C.C.M. on Lt. Farrell, J. Killed at Larelvan	
"	"	"	Lt. Garrison Leave U.K. 12/9/19. to 26.9.19.	
"	"	"	Capt. Pratt. M.P.L.T. 2nd Queens W. returned from Leave. U.K.	
"	"	"	Mr. D. Baker. S.C. returned from attachment 139.F.D.	
"	13/9/19	"	Pte Naylor. E.R. returned to Unit for Demobilisation	
"	14/9/19	"	"	
"	15/9/19	Raining	Pte Henderson. A. admitted 139.F.D.	
"	16/9/19	Fine	2/Sgt. Sgt. Lush. T.W. Leave U.K. 17/9/19 to 1.10.19. Home a/c H.P.	
"	"	"	Pte McCarthy returned to H.C. Sqd. Int. Town.	
"	"	"	London Dist. Horse Show Overall. Co. 1st Major, 2nd M. Cart.	
"	17/9/19	"	Pte Hunter + Pte Holloway returned and Coy. to M.T. Coy.	
"	18/9/19	"	L. Egerson A. Leave U.K. 19/9/19 to 3/1/19. Sgt Denny B.M. 6.J. Coy.	
"	19/9/19	Raining	Pte Turley, Lynch, Albert, Bagshaw and Burr. from 238 Emp.C.	
"	"	"	Capt. J. L. Egan-Bell, and Lt. Clayke, reported to Company.	

Army Form C. 2118.

WAR DIARY
or
INTELLIGENCE SUMMARY.
(Erase heading not required.)

Place	Date	Hour	Summary of Events and Information	Remarks and references to Appendices
Blac R	20/9/19		Month June. Lieut Gardner & Haviland C.E. 7 days C.E.	
"	"		Lt Cust & Lt Bunnell returned from leave U.K.	
"	"		Lt Heard, A.T. and Lt Mel. A.J. reported from leave U.K.	
"	21/9/19		Pte Lloyd E.P. been U.K. 22/9 to 6.6/19. Pte Tullis rel from leave U.K.	
"	"		Pte Edgar & T. Fowler to 17th R.F. Baggage.	
"	22/9/19		Pte Tullis J. returned to Unit for demobilization.	
"	"		Pte Torby adm H.P., Pte Marsden dis H.P.	
"	"		Pte Carroll & Pte Mee returned to 17th R.F.	
"	"		Pte Edgar G.R. & Pte Whaley E. transferred to R.R.O.	
"	23/9/19		Pte Cooper adm H.P. Pte Parker N. leave U.K. 24/9 to 8/10/19.	
"	24/9/19	Raining	Pte Page returned to Unit for demobilization	
"	"		Pte Ballard, Pte Kerry, Pte May, & Pte Bushell return to Depot.	
"	25/9/19	"	L/ Farrell J. discharged to P. Rifle Inspection (Comp Pay).	
"	26/9/19	Fine	Col. Marshall, Col. Noble, Lt Parr. Proceed for demobilization	
"	"		No 416. Coy ME Henry Stafft died in Italy.	
"	27/9/19	Raining	" Cpl Morgan Marshall R.A.V.C. completed H.D. No 416. Certificate from Force Record	

Army Form C. 2118.

WAR DIARY
or
INTELLIGENCE SUMMARY.
(Erase heading not required.)

Place	Date	Hour	Summary of Events and Information	Remarks and references to Appendices
Cher	27/9/19 (cont)		Weather Raining. Usual Rontine. Pte Cooper (alias HD) QM. Sergt. L. Wootten HP. V.P.G) Pass at Rotumo from Conv. U.K.	
"	28/9/19	"	Col Marshall Col. Miller St Lucia returned from Sunst Camp. Pte of No 416. Bay ashore dispatched to 52. M.V.S. Lt. L.E. Runnan reported from Conv. U.K.	
"	29/9/19	7	No 423. Ch/c. Gld. H.D. Clarke St. Kephion Camp. Pte Stansland P.E. attached to B. nuclei escort.	
"	30/9/19	"	Pte Young v Pte Luijo transferred to No 2 Company. " Chandra A returned to unit for Demobilization. Pte Lowell J admitted Hosp: (V.P.G)	

CAPT. O.G. No. 4 COMPANY
LONDON REGIMENT TRAIN

www.ingramcontent.com/pod-product-compliance
Lightning Source LLC
Chambersburg PA
CBHW081536160426
43191CB00011B/1772